THE
FAKE GOD
REFERENCE GUIDE

THE
FAKE GOD
REFERENCE GUIDE

YASMEEN SURI

XULON PRESS

Xulon Press
2301 Lucien Way #415
Maitland, FL 32751
407.339.4217
www.xulonpress.com

Copyright © 2018 by Yasmeen Suri

All rights reserved solely by the author. The author guarantees all contents are original and do not infringe upon the legal rights of any other person or work. No part of this book may be reproduced in any form without the permission of the author. The views expressed in this book are not necessarily those of the publisher.

Unless otherwise indicated, Scripture quotations taken from the Amplified Bible (AMP). Copyright © 1954, 1958, 1962, 1964, 1965, 1987 by The Lockman Foundation. Used by permission. All rights reserved.

Scripture quotations taken from the Contemporary English Version (CEV). Copyright © 1995 American Bible Society. Used by permission. All rights reserved.

Scripture quotations taken from the English Standard Version (ESV). Copyright © 2001 by Crossway, a publishing ministry of Good News Publishers. Used by permission. All rights reserved.

Scripture quotations taken from the King James Version (KJV) – *public domain*.

Scripture quotations taken from the New American Standard Bible (NASB). Copyright © 1960, 1962, 1963, 1968, 1971, 1972, 1973, 1975, 1977, 1995 by The Lockman Foundation. Used by permission. All rights reserved.

Scripture quotations taken from the Holy Bible, New International Version (NIV). Copyright © 1973, 1978, 1984, 2011 by Biblica, Inc.™. Used by permission. All rights reserved.

Scripture quotations taken from the New King James Version (NKJV). Copyright © 1982 by Thomas Nelson, Inc. Used by permission. All rights reserved.

Scripture quotations taken from the Holy Bible, New Living Translation (NLT). Copyright ©1996, 2004, 2007 by Tyndale House Foundation. Used by permission of Tyndale House Publishers, Inc.

Printed in the United States of America.

ISBN 9781545636770

Thank you Lord for giving me the patience and endurance to write this book.

May it accomplish Your will in the lives of men and women around the world
In Jesus Name, amen.

"But as for you, speak the things which are proper for sound doctrine."
Titus 2:1, NKJV

TABLE OF CONTENTS

Introduction ix
1. Contemplative (Centering) Prayer......................1
2. Christian Yoga 3
3. Soaking Prayer 7
4. Sozo Ministry...9
5. Holy Laughter 11
6. Spiritual Drunkenness................................... 13
7. Kundalini spirit 17
8. Meditation 19
9. Labyrinths... 21
10. Open Portals/Open Heavens 23
11. Angel Orbs.. 25
12. Spirit Travel/Out of Body Experiences.................. 27
13. Fire Tunnels 31
14. Visualization 33
15. Gold Dust/Glory Clouds............................... 35
16. Gems/Angel Feathers/Oil/Crystals..................... 37
17. Christian Mysticism...................................... 41
18. Yoga 43
19. Horoscopes/Astrology 47
20. Psychics.. 49
21. Palm Reading.. 51
22. Essential Oils 53
23. Karma 57
24. Reincarnation 59

25. Christ Consciousness 61
26. Reiki... 63
27. Holistic Medicine..................................... 65
28. Grave Soaking.. 67
29. Prophets/Divination 69
30. Female Angels 71
31. Name it, Claim it 73
32. Theophostics 75
33. The Third Eye 77
34. Hypnotism 79

INTRODUCTION

Now the serpent was more crafty than any of the wild animals the LORD God had made. He said to the woman, "Did God really say, 'You must not eat from any tree in the garden'? The woman said to the serpent, "We may eat fruit from the trees in the garden, but God did say, 'You must not eat fruit from the tree that is in the middle of the garden, and you must not touch it, or you will die.'" "You will not certainly die," the serpent said to the woman. "For God knows that when you eat from it your eyes will be opened, and you will be like God, knowing good and evil." (Genesis 3:1-5, NIV)

Since the fall of man, humans have been depraved apart from God and they have a desire to "be like God". This desire in our fallen nature, apart from Christ, yearns to do things "our way" and to become the "god" of our own lives. When we become the god of our own lives, we make our own rules, our feelings become our own moral compass and we make our own moral and spiritual laws. We try to fill our empty souls with anything and everything of the flesh. More money, sex, drinks, lies, immorality, self-righteousness, rules, religion, drugs, materialism, etc. will never satisfy the human heart. Churches across the world are compromising and allowing empty entertainment and motivational speeches that invite false teachers and teachings behind the pulpit. Where should we place our trust? Our trust should be in God's Word. Most Pastors and everyday

Christians are un-informed about these demonic, New Age, eastern mystical or counterfeit movements infiltrating the church. Jesus said there would be a great falling away from the faith and people will give heed to seducing spirits and doctrines of demons. This booklet will inform us of the dangers of the numerous teachings that are infiltrating the church at large.

We must remember that the enemy wants to fool us. The Bible says that he is crafty. He wants to take as many down as he can in the end times because he knows his time is short. We must warn each other and hold each other accountable in what we watch, listen to, and participate in. This is not the time to dance with the devil. If you give Satan an inch, he will take a mile. He comes to steal, kill and destroy from you. *"Be sober, be vigilant; because your adversary the devil walks about like a roaring lion, seeking whom he may devour." (1 Peter 5:8, NKJV)*

CONTEMPLATIVE (CENTERING) PRAYER

Proponents of the Contemplative prayer methodology are doing exactly what occultists and mystics have been doing for centuries, only now it is Christianized. Having its roots in eastern mysticism, contemplative prayer has made its inroads into the evangelical community. It has been practiced and promoted by Roman Catholic and Greek Orthodox monasticism. Also referred to as "centering" prayer, the idea is to find the center of your being by repeating a religious word as a mantra and trying to listen to the voice of God from within you as you wait in silence. Its advocates are false prophets whom you ought to beware of. For those who are not yet aware of what "the silence" is, "the silence", according to Buddhist, Hindu, Theosophist, Christian mystic, etc. literature is a self-induced altered state of consciousness one enters when practicing contemplative "centering" prayer. Referred to by occultists and Christian mystics alike, "the silence" is where individuals say they "commune with the Divine Consciousness", or the "Divine Self".

In actuality, "the silence" is an altered state of consciousness (Alpha state) whereby human beings, in a self-induced mystical way, interface spiritually with demonic entities that teach pantheistic (All-is-God, God-is-All) and pan-en-theistic (All-in-God) occult philosophy. Occult literature bears this out perfectly and this is why so many practitioners of Contemplative centering prayer end up believing an unbiblical, mysticism-friendly, Eastern occult worldview. Buddhist's, Theosophist's, Hindu's, Jain's, Witches, etc. do not come to the Biblical Jesus through Contemplative prayer. In fact, professing Christians can very easily erode their own personal Biblical view of God as a result of practicing the unbiblical Contemplative prayer centering method.

Self-induction into an altered state of consciousness is extremely dangerous. Christian mystics have done this through the centuries and they are doing it today. Hi-jacking Eastern spirituality (Buddhist, Hindu, etc.) in the name of Christianity, as a means to "connect with the Divine" and "have an experience", is evil. Yes, people are having "experiences" when they do these things but they are not "connecting" with the God of the Bible. Let the reader forever remember that the world of the occult is centered around spirituality based on experience, not on Biblical truth. Contrary to the schemes of the Prince of Darkness, the kingdom of our Lord, God and Savior Jesus Christ is based on worshipping God "in spirit and in truth". The Christian ought to remember that Satan is able to counterfeit spiritual experiences to such a degree that an undiscerning Christian can end up practicing Christianized occultism and Christianized Eastern mysticism. The definition of counterfeit is: "made in imitation of something else with intent to deceive".

"But you, when you pray, go into your room, and when you have shut your door, pray to your Father who is in the secret place; and your Father who sees in secret will reward you openly. And when you pray, do not use vain repetitions as the heathen do. For they think that they will be heard for their many words. Therefore do not be like them. For your Father knows the things you have need of before you ask Him." (Matthew 6: 6-8, NKJV)

CHRISTIAN YOGA

Christian websites and churches across the world are promoting this new synthesis of spirituality. We find that this movement is empowered mostly from women and those who do not esteem the word of God as they should.

One cannot play semantics with the Word of God and redefine its religious practice from Hinduism and cross it over to Christianity. Yoga is decidedly incompatible with Christianity, even with a Christian flavor. It is one thing to see Yoga adopted in the secular schools, but it is a totally different thing to see churches adopt it as part of their own curriculum for physical health and spiritual well being. Yoga is being incorporated into churches through teachers who know very little (some may know more) on what the real intent is. They believe it is complimentary to Christ's teachings and they are worshipping God in both body posture and prayer. I have been told by those who have lived in India, that if you offer Jesus to Hindu's, they have no problem adding Him to other gods they have. This does not justify a Christian who has only one God, to add other religious ways of devotion and worship to improve our spirituality.

We are being told how "neutral" the spiritual exercise of Yoga is and that people of all faiths can benefit by practicing Yoga without compromising their religious beliefs.

"...K.L. Seshagiri Rao, a professor of Hinduism at the University of Virginia and the editor of the Encyclopedia of Hinduism, said Yoga compliments all religions, adding that he has seen many Christians whose faith has been strengthened by their Yoga practice." "Yoga means *joining together. It's the joining of the individual spirit with the universal spirit,"* Rao said. *"No matter what religion you practice, you become a better person if you follow the principals of Yoga."*

In other words, the physical exercises and positions ("asanas"), along with the breathing techniques ("pranayama"), and meditation ("dhyana") were originally developed for VERY spiritual and religious reasons. The Bhagavad Gita testifies of it in over 50 verses, and certainly it would be difficult not to classify the Bhagavad Gita as a guide to Hindu religion.

Is adopting another religion's "spiritual practices" disobedient to the God who gave us the Bible? This is the crux of the whole matter. What Paul is saying is - look back at Israel's failures, the influences that came from the nations that surrounded them. They began to worship God with these nations' practices, and they were punished. We in the west need to define Yoga as the masters of Yoga in India define it. You cannot take another religion's practice and conform it to be sacred and spiritual for Jesus Christ. Jesus never mentioned it and he taught against practices like these, which deceive us into believing they are "good" for us.

Since Yoga is an ancient practice associated with and practiced in Hinduism and Buddhism, can we honestly walk with Jesus Christ and use it? What does light have to do with darkness? Did the Holy Spirit teach this, did He give this, did He command this; does He approve of this? Ask yourself honestly, are you being led by the Holy Spirit? Would He lead you to another religion's practice that He did not give? Eastern spiritual practices are to have no place in the church. This is really about 'inter-spirituality': the assimilation of values and spiritual practices of other religions into the church. This synthesizes all the beliefs which does two things; it introduces the church to other foreign and false spiritual beliefs and practices and removes one from a pure devotion to Jesus Christ. This is the influence of a progressive religious unity to bring together all faiths. One can trace this influence to those who are promoting interfaith and want this unity to take place. This is nothing to be naïve or indecisive about. For if you accept this you WILL eventually accept other practices as well. This then becomes the first step on the road to departing from the faith.

Paul explains to the believers, *"All things are lawful for me, but not all things are helpful; all things are lawful for me, but not all things edify."* (*1 Corinthians 10:23, NASB*) If you think you can adopt other religious/spiritual practices and not have it affect you adversely, think again, God says it will. Our example is none other than what God spoke to Israel- *Deut. 12:30-31: "take heed to yourself that you are not ensnared to follow them, after they are destroyed from before you, and <u>that you do not inquire after their gods</u>, saying, 'How did these nations serve their gods? I also will do likewise.'"<u>You shall not worship the LORD your God in that way</u>.*"

For what reason would Yoga be useful? Stretching? One can use other stretch poses outside of Yoga to make their blood flow. Hindus who practice Yoga are not doing it for stretching or to be more flexible. It is part of their spiritual practice to relieve them of their Karma and unite with the divine. Dave Hunt explains Yoga is, *"a Sanskrit word meaning to "yoke," and its aim is to yoke with the Hindu concept of God"* (Occult Invasion, p.220)

In answering the question "What is Yoga"? Swami Nirmalananda Giri states: *"Yoga" is a Sanskrit word that comes from the root-word yuj that means "to join." Yoga, then, is both union and the means to union. What do we join through Yoga? Two eternal beings: God, the infinite being, and the individual spirit that is finite being. In essence they are one, and according to Yogic philosophy all spirits originally dwelt in consciousness of that oneness."*

Yoga is ancient, but it is not the pathway the God of the Bible gave us to find Him. Incense was used as an act of worship; the similarity is that we are being told Yoga can be an act of worship, using the body. What we hear is that there is no conflict between Yoga and Christianity because this practice honors God by honoring one's body. Israel becomes our example: Jeremiah asks: *"Will the refreshing pure flowing waters be forsaken for strange waters?" Because My people have forgotten Me, they have burned incense to worthless idols. And they have caused themselves to stumble in their ways, from the ancient paths, to walk in pathways and not on a highway." (Jeremiah 18: 14-15 NKJV)*

Herein lies the problem; these Christians have abandoned the living water from Jesus Christ and have gone to broken cisterns, the world, and other religions to find refreshment. Never consulting the Word of whom Jesus said: *"Take My yoke upon you <u>and learn from Me</u>, for I am gentle and lowly in heart, and you will find rest for your souls." (Matt 11:29 NKJV)* Jesus also said, *"Now everyone who hears these sayings of Mine, and does not do them, will be like a foolish man who built his house on the sand." (Matt 7:26 NKJV)* The main reason anyone, even a Christian will search elsewhere, is because they are not building their life on God's Word. They have walked away from it. Once one does this, they become open to other religion's influences and philosophies that are contrary to Jesus Christ.

SOAKING PRAYER

"Soaking in the Spirit" and "Soaking Prayer", are terms which we often hear and they are being popularized by "Emergent" churches. Soaking was developed by the Toronto Airport Christian Fellowship (now Catch the Fire Toronto) which is also known as the "Toronto Blessing" and other unbiblical practices like holy laughter, drunk in the spirit and making animal sounds. This very popular practice is a modern form of contemplative prayer, where a person experiences and absorbs God's presence through stillness and by quieting or emptying one's mind, focusing on Jesus and opening up to the Holy Spirit, as he or she lies down and/or in a sitting position while listening to worship music. Although some choose to do this in total silence, like contemplative prayer, "soaking" focuses on having a mystical experience with God.

Just like all false doctrines, this cannot stand without twisting the Scriptures and taking them out of context. Those who practice soaking, always use twisted Scripture verses to justify that it is Biblical. They often use Psalm 46:10 which says *"Be still, and know that I am God..."*, or Matthew 6:6, *"But you, when you pray, enter into your closet, and when you have shut your door, pray to your Father which is in secret; and your Father which sees in secret shall reward you openly."* and Psalm 37: 7, *"Rest in the LORD, and wait patiently for Him..."*. The music used for soaking are usually quiet worship songs, but sometimes they also use soothing, relaxing instrumental worship music and believe me, when you hear this type of music, you will not be able to distinguish it from New Age music. In fact, if you look for it in the music store, most of this type of music is categorized under the New Age section. This music often has a melancholic feel to it which triggers a particular emotion or feeling. No wonder, most people who do soaking prayer often can't stop themselves from crying. As with contemplative prayer, transcendental meditation (TM), reiki, and Yoga, soaking requires that you empty your mind leading it to an altered state of consciousness (ASC) or trance. Those who practice soaking believe that they are inviting the presence of God or the Holy Spirit but in reality, what they are inviting is a different spirit. This is very dangerous because this gives familiar spirits an open invite for demonic attacks or worse, demonic possessions of the unsaved.

"Physical symptoms, which can include things like a tingling sensation that occur during Soaking Prayer, are similar to those experienced during the Kundalini experience, and both are dangerous and can take the practitioner into a demonic realm."

"Some of these phenomena are obvious: weeping, cries, exuberant and prolonged expressions of praise, shaking, trembling, calmness, bodily writhing and distortions, falling over (sometimes referred to as 'being slain in the Spirit'), laughter and jumping. Other phenomena are more subtle: slight trembling, fluttering of the eyelids, faint perspiring, a sheen on the face, ripples on the skin, deep breathing..." Wimber also said that people sometimes experience a sense of heaviness or tiredness, weeping or drunkenness." - "Soaking Prayer", Roger Harper

Soaking prayer, listening prayer, theophostics, or any other prayer that seeks the presence of God through mystical exercises is simply not Biblical. Biblical prayer is talking to God with His will in mind (1 John 5:14).

SOZO MINISTRY

Many churches are bringing a practice called SOZO into their ministry, at the peril of damaging the sheep and possibly shipwrecking their faith. SOZO Prayer is a technique based on psychology and used by so-called "inner healing ministries" sweeping churches today.

This psycho-spiritual deliverance and inner healing methodology is designed to exorcise demons from Christians. Not that a Christian *can* be possessed by demons, but that is one of many apostate teachings from the New Apostolic Reformation, or NAR.

During SOZO sessions, counselees receive help opening their minds to be filled with the Holy Spirit. They may be told that they have a spirit of Jezebel, or a Squid spirit, or some other creature or demon living inside of them. Once the demons are exorcised, their spirit-filled minds are now healed, and their broken connection to God is restored. Furthermore, SOZO counselors are taught to guide their clients (called "Sozoees"), through the "Five Doors" and "Father Ladder" concepts. The Five Doors through which demonic lies enter our brains are: Hatred, Sexual Sin, Occult (which SOZO actually *is*), Thievery and Fear.

The Berean Call describes Sozo thusly:

"*Although claiming to be Biblical, Sozo is a problem-solving approach based upon discovering root issues that are blocking spiritual growth. The issues supposedly reside in the subconscious memories of the individual and are identified as a person is regressed by the use of guided imagery and suggestion by the Sozo therapist. Of course, the Sozo therapist is trained to believe that the guided visualization is superintended by the Holy Spirit. This again is spiritualized psychotherapy, using techniques drawn from occult methodologies."*

Sozo is decidedly unbiblical and it is dangerous! Repressed memory therapy is extremely dangerous and has wreaked havoc on people's lives. Those seeking to be in the "presence of Jesus" will indeed find themselves in the company of an entity but it will not be the "Jesus" of the Bible. Remember *that "Satan himself masquerades as an angel of light." (2 Corinthians 11:14, ESV)*. Satan is the prince of darkness and well-meaning Christians will fall into the trap and deceitful workmen will also masquerade as "apostles of Christ."

The premise for this prayer is not Biblical. Where does the Bible teach us we need to root through our subconscious through the help of a Sozo minister in order to connect with God? Rather, we're told that anyone who wants to come to the Father can do so through the mediation of His Son (1 Timothy 2:5). If we want to connect with God, the Person you want to see is Jesus, not a Sozo minister. These people are not trained to handle the kind of potentially serious psychological issues that may arise during a typical session.

HOLY LAUGHTER

There are few within the charismatic evangelical Christian churches that have not heard of the term "holy laughter". These manifestations have been increasing across the world in the last several years at a rapid pace. Many churches are reporting spontaneous, uncontrollable laughter erupting from their congregations during the preaching of the Word of God. Some have even reported uncontrollable weeping, trance like states, people barking like dogs, animal noises and others unable to walk in a drunken like state. The Charismatic churches call it the "new outpouring" of the Holy Spirit.

The problem with this "new outpouring" is that it isn't very new at all. It has long been practiced by Islamic mystics, called dervishes, who would transfer it to their students by a touch or wave of the hand. The result would be uncontrolled laughter, weeping, convulsions, roaring, barking and hissing. In spite of these demonic noises and manifestations, the phenomenon is supposed to be a "revival" and a move of God.

Religious ecstasy (or *Kundalini)* was to be found in the mystery religions of the first century A.D. Back when the Corinth church seemed to be a hub of pagan Gnostic knowledge and ran rampant in unscriptural and immoral practices; the Greek mystery religions had prophets who babbled in unknown tongues which were caused by a *Kundalini* awakening.

A *Shaktipat* is where one person's *Kundalini* is awakened by another who already has had the experience. *Shaktipat* only raises the *Kundalini* temporarily but the demonic transference has taken place. This is what is going on in the churches; *Kundalini* is being transferred from one person to another – by blowing on someone, through baptismal water, laying on of hands, even holding ones hand over someone, but not touching them can begin a Shaktipat, etc.

There is no Biblical precedent for "holy" laughter. Laughter is rarely mentioned in the Bible. Yet, when it is, the Bible seems to make more of a case for holy sorrow than for "holy" laughter. Scripture supports Solomon's contention that "sorrow is better than laughter." It does not support the present "laughing revival." Substituting the word joy for laughter is a non sequitur. It is inaccurate and misleading. There is no scriptural authority for equating Biblical references to joy with the involuntary manifestations of "holy" laughter. Just because there are insufficient Bible texts to make the case for "holy" laughter, it does not follow that you can simply redefine the word "laughter" by substituting the word "joy". "Holy" laughter advocates rarely, if ever, discuss the need to "test the spirits." The Bible warns us that not every supernatural manifestation is necessarily from God. 1 John 4:1(KJV) says, *"Beloved, believe not every spirit, but try the spirits whether they are of God; because many false prophets are gone out into the world."* "Holy" laughter advocates rarely, if ever, talk about the Spirit's express warning that in the latter times some people will be supernaturally seduced by deceptive evil spirits into following them and not the one true God. 1 Timothy 4:1(KJV) warns, *"Now the Spirit speaketh expressly, that in the latter times some shall depart from the faith, giving heed to seducing spirits, and doctrines of devils."*

SPIRITUAL DRUNKENNESS

About 25 years ago, a worldwide revival movement broke out among Charismatic and Pentecostals, which was supposed to bring new life and blessing to the declining churches, through mysticism, spiritual experience and especially through a phenomenon called "spiritual drunkenness". It was alternately known as "The Laughing Revival", "The Toronto Blessing", and "The Brownsville Revival". The false revival leaders usually cite the account of the outpouring of the Holy Spirit on the day of Pentecost, as a justification for this false experience;

"And when the day of Pentecost was fully come, they were all with one accord in one place. And suddenly there came a sound from heaven as of a rushing mighty wind, and it filled all the house where they were sitting. And there appeared unto them cloven tongues like as of fire, and it sat upon each of them And they were all filled with the Holy Ghost, and began to speak with other tongues, as the Spirit gave them utterance."(Acts 2:1-4, NKJV)

Indeed the Pentecostal experience is in the Bible, and it occurred as a "sign and a wonder" to Israel exactly as Joel and the other prophets predicted. But there was no spiritual drunkenness or simulations of inebriated behavior in this account. But when Peter stood up to explain by Scripture what was occurring, some bystanders mocked the Apostles, accusing them of drunkenness.

"And they were all amazed, and were in doubt, saying one to another, What meaneth this? Others mocking said, These men are full of new wine." (Acts 2:12-13, KJV)

Notice the accusation of drunkenness was not serious. The Bible tells us that they were "mocking" when they accused the Apostles of being drunk. There was no behavior which suggested drunkenness. The real meaning of "spiritual drunkenness" is that it is a judgment from God himself on unfaithful people. *Isaiah 28:7-8 (NKJV) "But they also have erred through wine, and through strong drink are out of the way; the priest and the prophet have erred through strong drink, they are swallowed up of wine, they are out of the way through strong drink; they err in vision, they stumble in judgment. For all tables are full of vomit and filthiness, so that there is no place clean."*

Notice, it is the strong drink and the wine that caused the people to err, and go out of the way. Even the priest and the prophet "err in vision and stumble in judgment." I believe an extremely important thing to note is that much of the leadership of this "Mystical Revival" are composed of those who consider themselves to be "prophets". Even if it were true that they are prophets, Isaiah warns us that those who participate in this become blind and go into error!

Isaiah is even stronger in his denunciation of this in his next chapter:

"Stay yourselves, and wonder; cry ye out, and cry: they are drunken, but not with wine, they stagger, but not with strong drink. For the Lord hath poured out upon you the spirit of deep sleep, and hath closed your eyes: the prophets and your rulers, the seers hath he covered. And the vision of all is become unto you as the words of a book that is sealed, which men deliver to one that is learned, saying, Read this, I pray thee: and he saith, I cannot: for it is sealed: And the book is delivered to him that is not learned, saying Read this, I pray thee; and he saith, I am not learned. Wherefore the Lord said, Forasmuch as this people draw near me with their mouth, and with their lips do honour me, but have removed their heart far from me, and their fear toward me is taught by the precept of men: Therefore, behold, I will proceed to do a marvellous work among this people, even a marvellous work and a wonder: for the wisdom of their wise men shall perish, and the understanding of their prudent men shall be hid." (Isaiah 29:9-14, KJV)

There are several remarkable details in this passage that I would like to emphasize:

Verse 9 is a strong teaching that it is spiritual drunkenness and not alcoholism that is being condemned in this passage.

Verse 10 tells us that this is a judgment, from the Lord, upon us, our "prophets," rulers and seers. The judgment consists of blindness, slumber, and staggering drunkenness, especially on leaders. What really throws many people off these days is the fact that in many cases, seemingly sound, solid, respectable leadership are suddenly endorsing all of this as a move of God. Others may not endorse it, but are extremely reluctant to cry out against it. Now would be the "shining hour" for a group like the "Assemblies of God" and other Christian Pentecostal denominations to rise up and offer true leadership, as in days past, and soundly and scripturally take a stand against this heresy.

Verses 11-12 teach us that confusion, indecisiveness and inability to understand have brought us to the point where even learned men aren't sure what the Bible says, even though the people look for leadership. Eventually, the Bible is delivered to unlearned people, as verse 12 says. Notice that the unlearned don't refuse to teach, they just say, "I am not learned."

Is "knowing" the Scriptures mere theory, as opposed to revelation? This is called setting up a straw man so you can boldly kick it down, and this is what these teachers do all of the time. They posture themselves as champions for "revelation knowledge" and cast those who want to be doctrinally scrupulous as dried up, highly educated, "dead heads". Jesus made no such distinction. It was He who said, *"You do err, not knowing the Scriptures or the power of God."(Matthew 22:29, KJV)* To Him, knowing the Scriptures was equated with knowing the power of God!

THE KUNDALINI SPIRIT

Evil spirits such as "Kundalini" in Yoga and occult mysticism are dangerous spirits entering Christian churches in North America. These spirits are prophetic, offer visions, dreams, and feelings of peace. They can even look like the Holy Spirit. Only the most discerning are able to recognize these false spirits.

Kundalini is a demonic spirit which is known as a COUNTERFEIT Holy Spirit. Persons under the influence of this demonic spirit will testify to having "deep spiritual sensations" such as "knowing" other people's thoughts, outer body feelings of bliss and ecstasy, uncontrollable physical sensations such as crying, laughing, jerking, vivid dreams, visions, trances, etc. The Kundalini spirit gained access to the Western world from India through Hinduism, Yoga and New Age teachings. Don't for a minute think that Yoga is harmless. Yoga is an inherent part of Hindu philosophy which teaches man and nature are one with divinity. "Awakening the Kundalini" is the expression used by mystics, Hindu gurus and New Agers for the practice of focusing on a *serpent spirit* which, they say, resides in each one of us in the form of a coiled snake located at the base of the spine. Through meditation and physical body positioning, the aim is to *'raise the Kundalini'* through a total of seven spiritual waypoints – called 'Chakras' – located along the spine.

Shakti is always available to be experienced in our physical body as a series of currents, with seven focal points called chakras. A powerful concentration of Shakti known as Kundalini lies dormant at the base of everyone's spine. Numerous spiritual techniques can arouse

Kundalini and channel it upward through the chakras, awakening one into unity consciousness. The human body is conceived differently in Christianity: on the one hand created in the image of God, yet it is also the means of transmitting original sin and lays a person open to "evil spirits".

In Hinduism, the guru helps awaken the disciple's Kundalini and integrate the experience into ordinary life. Kundalini-like manifestations have occurred sporadically among Christians, but mainstream churches treat them as aberrations and even as the work of the devil. Those who have such experiences are conditioned to doubt their own sanity and are often regarded as mentally ill and even institutionalized. When you see videos of these "kriyas" or other Kundalini-type manifestations, you would often swear that you are watching a modern "Impartation"-type church meeting. (And I say this as someone who believes strongly in the gifts of the Holy Spirit. I just don't believe in "alien" anointing infiltrating the Body of Christ! There is a big difference between Kundalini and the real Holy Spirit).

A foreign spirit has been allowed to invade the church - first through Rodney Howard-Browne's ministry - then Toronto, then the Prophetic movement and on into Lakeland and many other ministries and movements. I urge people now to "test the spirits" just as we are commanded to in Scripture. Do not let just anyone lay hands on you. This is a powerful spirit and it has the backing of a lot of big-name ministries. In fact, these men and women are the very ones responsible for allowing it to spread right through the body of Christ. One day they will be answering to God for doing so. We are specifically warned in the Bible that the last days will be a time of seducing spirits, false prophets, lying signs and wonders, and that we always need to watch for "angels of light" masquerading as the real thing. Why does the modern church not take these warnings seriously? Aren't we living in the very days that the Bible warns about?

MEDITATION

With meditation being prescribed by doctors to relieve stress and spiritual leaders touting meditation as a way of spiritual growth, more and more Christians are becoming interested in this practice but are concerned as to whether it goes against their Christian faith. However, Christian and eastern meditation are very different in both their objectives and methods. Any form of meditation, apart from Biblical meditation, is opening the door wide to the enemy. Eastern meditation empties the mind. Biblical meditation fills the mind and spirit with God's Word. Emptying our mind is actually a very dangerous thing because it gives the enemy room to fill it with his deception. However, the Hebrew word for meditation actually means to speak or mutter, a practice that actually does the opposite of Eastern meditation. It fills our mind with God's Word and builds our spirit.

Eastern meditation focuses on self: centering yourself, your inner self, self actualization, breathing, physical feelings and emotions. The enemy will do anything to get us to stop focusing on Christ. Furthermore, his ultimate deception is pride or elevation of self. Biblical meditation takes our focus off of ourselves and places our focus on Jesus Christ. Eastern meditation seeks to relieve stress. The problem with our culture isn't stress. Stress is only a symptom of a deeper problem: Pride. Worry, fear, perfectionism ... these all have their root in pride and all result in stress. But God wants us to daily walk in faith that brings us peace no matter our circumstance. Jesus said, *"Peace I leave with you. My peace I give to you; not as the world gives do I give to you. Let not your heart be troubled, neither let it be afraid." (John 14:27, KJV)*

Christians absolutely shouldn't turn to anything other than Jesus Christ for the peace that will help to ease whatever it is that has brought stress on in their lives! Eastern meditation focuses on man being in control. Eastern meditation practices rely on self as the agent to bring peace, tranquility and oneness with deity—the original lie: "You can become like God." Biblical meditation reminds us God is almighty and when He is in control we can be at complete peace knowing that His purposes will prevail. Eastern meditation dethrones God and puts fallen man in His place. Eastern meditation is only escapism. By seeking higher levels of consciousness or altered states of consciousness, you can escape your stress and enter new realms of oneness with deity. But the fact remains that once we have returned to our usual state of consciousness, the stress is still there. Biblical meditation doesn't give us an escape from reality, it gives us supernatural strength through the Holy Spirit to walk through the "fire and flood" at peace, knowing that God is in control of every situation. We don't need to escape our troubles; by faith we walk through them, counting it all joy, knowing that the testing of your faith produces patience.

Eastern meditation manipulates circumstances to bring peace. By using atmosphere, objects, silence, breathing techniques and more, people are able to enter a meditative state. It's a manipulation of circumstances and atmosphere. However, the child of God can meditate on God's Word whenever, wherever, no matter the situation or circumstance because we have direct access to the throne of God. Indeed, we are the temple of God and His Holy Spirit dwells within us. We never need to manipulate any situation to experience peace; we simply recall the precious promises of the Word of God and place our faith and trust in Him!

LABYRINTHS

Labyrinths are pagan instruments used as occult gateways into the supernatural. Most think of a labyrinth as a maze that's easy to get lost in with winding paths and dead ends. A Labyrinth is different than a maze because it is a winding path. For the spiritually discerning, the Labyrinth is nothing more than occult paganism masquerading itself as another form of Christian prayer.

The prayer Labyrinth, also known as a meditation Labyrinth, is used for prayer, religious, mystical rituals, initiations, and for spiritual growth say New Age disciples. Labyrinth prayer walks are not Biblical nor should they be used within the Christian faith. Those that teach their use offer them as "another type of prayer, or prayer in motion."

We are not talking about a Christian praying to the God of the Bible while walking down the sidewalk. No, this is occult spiritualism. To New Age disciples, a Labyrinth represents the "path of life". As one travels the Labyrinth's path of life, it leads their walk to the center of an intricate design representing the center of oneself then exiting along the same path. A prayer or meditation Labyrinth only has one route or a single path. Again, unlike the maze, a Labyrinth is designed with one destination and is impossible to get lost within.

THE LABYRINTH SOCIETY

According to the Labyrinth Society, their vision is to "activate and facilitate the transformation of the human spirit." They also use the prayer Labyrinth as "a personal practice for healing and growth, a tool for community building, an agent for global peace, and a metaphor for life."

These Labyrinth groups offer workshops about the Labyrinth for "divine imprint, mystical tradition, as a sacred path and gateway." It's surely a gateway, an occult gateway and used by New Age practitioners to transcend into an altered state of consciousness. In that state, they believe in becoming one with the divine universe. After one's "centering," they can exit the Labyrinth to take their newly found spiritual awakening and revelation to the world.

Those promoting prayer and meditation Labyrinths wrongly use a Catholic cathedral, not Bible Scripture, as historical precedent for their use because the medieval "Cathedral of Our Lady of Chartres" outside Paris, France has a prayer Labyrinth. Chartres removes their sanctuary chairs once a month exposing its Labyrinth on the floor to attract pilgrims that walk the Labyrinth with their heads bowed in prayer.

The prayer Labyrinth path has three stages - the inward journey, the center, and the outward journey. There is nothing wrong with walking down the street of your city in prayer. Using a prayer Labyrinth is very different. Hinduism teaches that life is on a path, and to some, the Labyrinth is a model of that path. So for New Age practitioners a Labyrinth meditation walk is a metaphor for the journey to the center of your deepest self and back out into the world with an enlightened awareness of who you are. The Apostle Paul said, *"Follow me as I follow Christ." (1 Cor 11:1, NIV)* Nowhere in Scripture did the apostles teach disciples to find themselves in a prayer Labyrinth. Jesus instructed his disciples to die to self-saying, *"For whosoever will save his life shall lose it: and whosoever will lose his life for my sake shall find it." (Matthew 16:25, KJV)*

OPEN PORTALS/OPEN HEAVENS

This heresy teaches that there are geographic locations on Earth that possess super-spiritual access to the heavenlies. A corollary doctrine teaches that intercessors can open up portals to the heavens by cleansing geographic areas of demonic spirits, including ancestral or territorial powers and principalities. The modern prophetic and apostolic false prophets in the Church are forever coming up with teachings that are a distortion of the true meaning of the Word. What are these "portals" they are talking about? The New Apostolic Reformation, with their mystics, psychics, and false prophets, have been teaching a distorted interpretation to Jacob's dream, and have created a doctrine about heavenly portals and an "Open Heaven". Based on an explanation by John Paul Jackson, there is an:

"...existence of portals--doors and passageways--leading to and from the heavenly realms. When you are standing in a portal, it feels like an open Heaven. A heavenly portal is a spherical opening of light that offers divine protection by which angels and heavenly beings can come and go, without demonic interference. God has designed portals to begin in the third Heaven, travel through the second Heaven, and open upon Earth."

As you can see, a lot of liberty has been taken to create this teaching. We have no scriptural evidence to prove that angelic activity occurs in these portals, or if it is demonic alone. But there is one thing that each of these portal/vortex locations have in common - paganism. We know that these locations were used in pagan worship by the Incas in Peru, the Egyptians at the Great Pyramid of Giza,

Druids at Stonehenge in the UK, Indians at Sedona in Arizona, along with many others. Each of these pagan groups have pierced the veil between realities to seek an "experience" in a higher spiritual realm, or to gain understanding.

Where can they be found in the Bible? The answer is nowhere. But the idea of portals to heaven is very much a New Age concept. The concept of "portals" is to be found in the heretical Pseudepigrapha book called the Book of Enoch, which are obviously not the original writings of Enoch. The Catholics believe that Mary, whom they call the "Immaculate Virgin Mary", "Queen Of Heaven" and "Mother Of God", is endowed with the keys to *"open to us the portals of heaven"*. On a New Age site, a deluded New Ager claims that "I have ascended through the Portals of Heaven where I established my rebirth in the earth itself, and now have taken my rightful place in the Kingdom of Heaven." The Bible says nothing about portals to heaven. The only portal to heaven for human beings is through the blood of Jesus Christ. Many New Agers speak about opening portals to let the "Ascended Masters" through and even some people are trying to open portals to let alien beings through. The Bible never speaks about opening portals but the occult clearly does.

The Bible states that false prophets are driven by *"false visions and delusion of their minds (Jer 14:14)."* Then we have this "open heaven" taught by a number of "Latter Rain" false teachers and false prophets. There is no such thing. This third heaven is only "open" to those who have died in Christ. God works with His church but the access they have to heaven is through prayer in Christ, who intercedes for us with the Father. But the core issue is that people are trying to come under the false apostles and get squarely into the center of the "Dominion" doctrines of the NAR(New Apostolic Reformation).

ANGEL ORBS

Many people have been puzzled by the appearance of "orbs"—spherical spots of light—in their photographs. These orbs can be various sizes, but usually they are small, white and round. Most significantly, orbs are not apparent to the naked eye; they only show up in pictures and sometimes on video. Some people view orbs as evidence of paranormal or supernatural activity in a "haunted" location. Many others, including Christians, have a different perspective on the existence of orbs.

Some ghost chasers and paranormal investigators claim that orbs are manifestations of departed human spirits. They say that, as some ghosts seek to communicate with the living, the ghosts will exert psychic energy to make their presence visible, at least on film. From a Christian point of view, this theory has a major problem: there are no such things as ghosts, in the sense of "departed spirits of once-living humans." The Bible teaches that, when a person dies, he or she is immediately in one of two places, heaven or hell (Luke 16:22–23). There is no time for "wandering" or "haunting." There *are* spirits in this world, however—unclean spirits (demons) and holy spirits (angels).

Some Christians believe that orbs are real. If they see an orb in a picture taken inside their home, they conclude that there are spirits in the house. If they believe the spirits to be demonic, they might call a pastor or priest over to "cleanse" the house or pray through the rooms. If they believe the orbs are good, they might take comfort in the fact that God has sent His angels to watch over them. Again, from a Biblical perspective, these theories have a problem. The Bible never mentions orbs. It never hints that spirits, good or bad, will manifest themselves to us as spherical globs of light. We have no reason to believe that our modern technology can coax a spirit to make itself visible. The belief that an orb is an angel or demon "caught on film" is based on ideas that do not come from the Bible.

There is a logical explanation for orbs. Orbs are almost always photographed 1) indoors, 2) using a flash, 3) on a digital camera, 4) with a low-resolution lens. These facts have led many to conclude that orbs are, in reality, dust particles floating between the camera and the subject of the photograph. The theory is that these airborne particles reflect the light of the camera's flash. They appear blurry or transparent because they are out of focus; they are not visible to the naked eye because they must be illuminated by the flash. Other small particles in the air, such as pollen, rain, or snow, can produce the same "orbs."

Our belief in the supernatural does not come from photographic "proof" but from the Word of God. The Bible is our guide. Whether or not orbs have a supernatural origin does not change the fact that a Christian is to love God fearlessly, keep his eyes on Jesus, and be filled with the Spirit. *"The one who is in you is greater than the one who is in the world." (1 John 4:4, NIV)*

SPIRIT TRAVEL/OUT OF BODY EXPERIENCES

Information about the "out-of-body" experience is both vast and subjective. According to Wikipedia, one out of ten people claim to have had an out-of-body experience (OBE), and there are many different types of the experiences claimed. They range from involuntary out-of-body experiences or near-death experiences that happen after or during a trauma or accident, to what is called "astral projection" in which a person voluntarily tries to leave his/her body behind and ascend to a spiritual plane where he/she believes he/she will find truth and clarity.

A few famous Christians have had what might be called, in today's world, an out-of-body experience, most notably the Apostle Paul. He says in 2 Corinthians 12:1-4 (ESV), *"I must go on boasting. Although there is nothing to be gained, I will go on to visions and revelations from the Lord. I know a man in Christ who fourteen years ago was caught up to the third heaven. Whether it was in the body or out of the body I do not know—God knows. And I know that this man—whether in the body or apart from the body I do not know, but God knows—was caught up to paradise. He heard inexpressible things, things that man is not permitted to tell."* In the verses preceding this passage, Paul lists his "boasts" or the things that, if he were counting on works and good deeds to secure his salvation, would get him into heaven. Though he seems to be referring to a third party, scholars agree that he is speaking of himself in the third person. Therefore, he is including this apparent out-of-body experience in his list of boasts. The point he is making is that any revelation that comes from outside the Bible (extra-Biblical revelation) is not a reliable source, and as Paul says, "There is nothing to be gained by it." This does not mean that his out-of-body experience wasn't real, only that he is not relying on it to give him truth or really to benefit himself or other people in any way.

An involuntary out-of-body experience or a near-death experience, like the Apostle Paul's, should be treated in the same way as a dream in the life of a Christian—an unexplained phenomenon that may make a good story, but does not give us truth. The only place we find absolute truth is in the Word of God. All other sources are merely subjective human accounts or interpretations based on what we can discover with our finite minds. The book of Revelation, or John's vision, is an exception to this, as are the prophecies or visions of the Old Testament prophets. In each of those cases, the prophets were told that this was a revelation from the Lord, and they should share what they had seen because it was directly from the mouth of God.

A voluntary out-of-body experience, or an "astral projection," is a different story. A person trying to achieve an out-of-body experience in order to connect with spirits or the spirit world is practicing the occult. There are two forms of this. The first is called the "phasing" model, in which the person tries to find new spiritual truth by accessing a part of the mind that is "shut off" during everyday life. This practice is connected to Buddhism or postmodernism and the belief that enlightenment is achieved from looking within oneself. The other form, called the "mystical" model, is when the person tries to exit the body entirely, his/her spirit traveling to another plane that is not connected to the physical world at all.

The Bible explicitly warns against occult practice, or sorcery, in Galatians 5:19-20 (ESV), saying that *"those who practice it will not inherit God's kingdom"*. God's commands are always for our good, and He commands us to stay far away from occult practices because there is great potential, when trying to access the spiritual world, of opening oneself up to demons who can tell us lies about God and confuse our minds. In Job 4:12-21, Eliphaz describes being visited by a lying spirit in a vision that tells him God does not regard humans and that He doesn't care for us, which is false! The phasing model is also futile, according to Scripture. Jeremiah 17:9 (ESV) says, *"The heart is deceitful above all things and desperately sick; who can understand it?"* and 1 Corinthians 2:1-5(ESV) says, *"When I came to you, brothers, I did not come with eloquence or superior wisdom as I proclaimed to you the testimony about God. For I resolved to know nothing while I was with you except Jesus Christ and him crucified. I came to you in weakness and fear, and with much trembling. My message and my preaching were not with wise and persuasive words, but with a demonstration of the Spirit's power, so that your faith might not rest on men's wisdom, but on God's power."* It is futile to search for infinite wisdom inside the finite mind of man.

One concrete example of this comes from the popular book *90 Minutes in Heaven* by Pastor Don Piper. Piper describes what is, in essence, an out-of-body experience he had after a severe car accident, during which he believes he died and went to heaven for ninety minutes. Whether or not Piper did actually see heaven or spend time there is debatable, and in the end nobody but God knows. However, there is a serious problem, theologically speaking, with the conclusion Pastor Piper draws from his experience. He tells the reader that, now that he has "been to heaven," he can speak comfort to grieving people at funerals "with more authority" than he could previously. Piper's motives are correct: he wants to give people hope. However, it is dead wrong to say that his own subjective experience will give him more authority to administer the hope of heaven than the perfect truth of Scripture would do.

In conclusion, whatever sort of out-of-body experience we are talking about, the main point to remember is that an out-of-body experience will give us neither truth nor knowledge. If an involuntary out-of-body experience occurs in the life of a Christian, the best approach would be to consider it in the same category as a dream—interesting, perhaps, but not a source of truth. Christians are to find truth only in the words of God, as Jesus prays in John 17:17(ESV), *"Sanctify them in the truth; Your word is truth."*

FIRE TUNNELS

For those who have never heard of these practices, a fire tunnel is when a group of people line up opposite one another to form a kind of tunnel through which worshippers pass. As they do so, the people forming the tunnel lay hands on them and impart the "Holy Spirit" to them. People who have walked a tunnel may experience manifestations known in revivalist circles as being "drunk in the Spirit" in which a person looks, acts and feels as if they are drunk.

Laying on of hands to impart an anointing of the Holy Spirit is Biblical. *"When Paul placed his hands on them, the Holy Spirit came on them, and they spoke in tongues and prophesied" (Acts 19:6, ESV).* *"Whom they set before the apostles: and when they had prayed, they laid their hands upon them" (Acts 6:6, ESV).* *"Then laid they their hands on them, and they received the Holy Spirit" (Acts 8:17-19, ESV).*

It's not the laying on of hands that are suspect; it's what kind of anointing this gesture is supposedly transferring. In some renewal and revival movements, these "gifts" of the Spirit can be quite bizarre, such as uncontrollable laughter (called Holy Laughter), staggering, swooning, going through the motions of childbirth supposedly to "birth" a new ministry, stripping off one's clothes (called Holy Nakedness) and a variety of other manifestations. Some Protestant leaders believe churches that promote these kinds of manifestations are associated with what they like to call the "Third Wave" movement which is based on the belief that there have been three recent periods of activity of the Holy Spirit in recent years.

The first was the Pentecostal revival around 1906, the second was the Charismatic movement of the 1960s and the third began in the 1980s with a new commitment to signs, wonders and supernatural experiences with God," writes John Wolf, founder of the Church Education Resource Ministries.

"Do not quench the Spirit. Do not despise prophetic utterances. Test everything; retain what is good. Refrain from every kind of evil." (1 Thess 5:19, NKJV)

The best way to do this is to test everything against Scripture. You'll often hear someone say that the Spirit is "doing something new" in this or that church and therefore it can't be checked against Scripture. Beware! The reason why there is no Scriptural basis for angel feathers falling from the ceiling or people's teeth turning gold is not because it's "something new" but because it's something false. Another way to do this is to look for the fruit of the Spirit. This is what Jesus meant when He taught *"By their fruits you will know them." (Matt 7:16, KJV)*

In other words, as we mature in the faith and the following of Christ, we no longer pine for religious "experiences", but for a closer union with God. Our tastes have changed. It's no longer the flesh and all of its persistent demands that drives us; it's the Spirit of peace and self-control. We are gentler, more loving people, patient with others and generous of heart. Jesus' command to *"love one another as I love you" (John 15:12, ESV)* has become the rule of our life.

VISUALIZATION

New Age visualization claims to work by using the mind to influence one's perceptions and personal reality. Proponents claim that by properly controlling each person's alleged mental power, they can influence and change a person's ideas, consciousness, and even his or her physical and spiritual environment.

For example, visualization can supposedly be used to change one's self-image from negative to positive by holding a positive image of oneself in the mind. Visualization may also serve to uncover a claimed "inner divinity" that can allegedly manipulate reality. By creating the proper mental image and environment and then holding it or projecting it outward, practitioners claim they can exercise mental power over every aspect of their lives. Related practices are also used in magic ritual to call on spirits in order to secure such goals.

Most of the popular "think yourself rich" (or healthy, sexy, happy, etc.) seminars and texts endorse and use visualization. Modern New Age seminars, such as Silva Mind Control and the Forum (formerly "est"), collectively have millions of graduates, on whom they have used varying visualization techniques. In one's mind, one can create "projection screens" on which to picture desired images — whether seeing oneself with greater self-confidence, learning abilities, or less weight, or imagining one's white blood cells warding off viral invaders or specific illnesses.

In *The Seduction of Christianity*, author Dave Hunt devotes two chapters to the harmful influence of visualization within the church. He observes, "'Visualization' and 'Guided Imagery' have long been recognized by sorcerers of all kinds as the most powerful and effective methodology for contacting the spirit world in order to acquire supernatural power, knowledge and healing. Such methods are neither taught nor practiced in the Bible as helps to faith or prayer." Faith is rarely placed in the Biblical God or Christ but rather in one's own alleged inner powers, mental capacity, or "intuitive" abilities; or in cosmic energy, the universe, and so forth. Christians are to be renewed daily by the Holy Spirit, prayer, and the Word of God. They are not to be renewed by a transpersonal psychology using Eastern metaphysics or inner work through visualization. The power of the Word of God to build a truly integrated person makes modern visualization pale by contrast. Jesus said, *"Apart from me you can do nothing." (John 15:5, NIV)* The Bible does not teach or give examples of mystical experiences to draw near to God. We cannot bring ourselves closer to God through a technique or fantasized trip but are brought near God through Christ (Jn. 16:24, Eph. 2:13, I Tim. 2:5).

Mental imaging is a common practice in the occult. One holds an image in their mind and puts in the details like coloring in an outline. As they envision it each day, meditate on it, it becomes clearer and will come to pass. This technique is now used for healing traumas that are emotional, cancer and other diseases. One sees the cancer or disease being fought and conquered and essentially leaving. While mentally rehearsing Scripture and using pictures in our mind for Biblical accounts can be useful, it is not the same as attempting to create spiritual reality, or to cause through any mind technique such as positive thinking. To change, alter, or create reality you are then entering the realm of sorcery.

GOLD DUST/GLORY CLOUDS

Modern charismatics speak of a glory cloud as a regular occurrence, sometimes with gold dust (which has never been proven to be actual gold) during a church service. Videos have been taken inside various churches, showing a cloud of smoke filling the building. This is said to be the glory of God and the presence of God. Without going into much scriptural argument in this article, I would just like to point out that smoke can be easily filtered into a building by many means. It's really not that difficult. Secondly, and more importantly, have you not read the Bible and seen how great men of God in Scripture have reacted to being in the presence of God? Moses turned white! Ezekiel, Paul on the Damascus road, John in the first chapter of Revelation... these men all fell face down in fear and trembling (in their right minds, mind you, not in some kind of drunken glory) at being in the presence of holiness. Gold dust from various churches has been taken and analyzed under microscope and found to be nothing more than gold colored confetti available from any stationery store. I have heard stories of people filling their hair with this glitter in the bathrooms before going out into the church and claiming to have been blessed with this "manifestation".

The Scriptures reveal that God thinks highly of gold. He compares His own word *to "fine gold"* (Psalm 19:10). When He instructed Moses on the building of the tabernacle, God gave specific directions about the use of pure gold, pure silver, and precious stones (Numbers 8:4; Exodus 28:17–21; 37:17–22). God required the genuine articles because the purity of precious metals and stones reflects His own value and worth. In fact, God is repulsed by counterfeits or anything impure (Exodus 30:3; Ezekiel 22:18; Isaiah 1:25). So when we examine the Scriptures as the Bereans did, do we find there a God who would manifest His glory with imitation gold dust and plastic gems? This phenomenon does not appear to harmonize with God as He has revealed Himself to us through His Word. 1 John 4:1 commands us to "test the spirits to see whether they are from God, because many false prophets have gone out into the world." So how do we test something like falling gold dust? A cursory Google search indicates that at no time has any worshipper showered in gold dust ever produced any genuine gold.

Leviticus 10:1 describes the fire that Nadab and Abihu offered as "unauthorized". The King James Version renders it as "strange fire". It also says that the fire they offered was not commanded by the Lord. This offering can be understood as being a picture of our worship meetings today, and how we conduct ourselves in God's house and offer up worship to God. It is not the purpose of this book to malign or question the integrity of anyone who has experienced a "gold dusting", but it would seem that the Bible stands in sharp contrast to the claims of those who advocate such displays. There are no manifestations of this sort recorded anywhere in the Bible. Even during the powerful apostolic days of the book of Acts, God's glory was revealed in the *transformed lives* of those who called upon Jesus' name. The apostles' miracles were merely to promote the resurrected Christ and were not an end in themselves. At no time did anyone report the appearance of a plastic glitter cloud as evidence of the Holy Spirit among them (1 Corinthians 2:2; Acts 3:12).

.

GEMS/ANGEL FEATHERS/ OIL/CRYSTALS

Many "strange" signs and wonders that happen in some Charismatic church gatherings–things like feathers and gemstones falling out of the air, the appearance of what seems to be "manna" (the bread the Israelites ate in the desert), people receiving gold teeth, and people being spontaneously covered in gold dust or oil. Some Pastors convince people that these signs are from God and the Holy Spirit and our present understanding of Scripture cannot take us far enough. They say that laughter, gold dust, oil and a cloud (appearing in the church building) are also signs of God's presence. They also believe that these signs and manifestations "are simple indicators of God's presence and purpose". They call these signs God's "personal notes" to us. When evaluating the use of crystals for healing purposes, it is important to be aware of the fact that the majority of experts who promote crystal healing are involved in the occult. The word occult means 'hidden'. Occultism concerns itself with the study and utilization of supernatural influences, powers and phenomena that are normally hidden from the regular physical senses, and are generally considered to be outside the realm of traditional scientific observation. Occultists believe that human beings, and the world in which we live, are permeated by invisible mystical energies. They believe that these energies can be focused and directed by 'sacred stones', such as crystals and other talismans, so as to induce physical healing and spiritual enlightenment.

The "precious stones" or "gems" that have "fallen from heaven" appeared have all proved to be imitation. The Pharisees were an ancient sect of Judaism who were very lax and liberal (as opposed to strict and conservative) when it came to written Scripture and Bible interpretation, nullifying God's Word while adding on their own clever and deceptive twists, rules and "traditions of men" (see Mark 7:13). They went "off the map" of truth and put their twisted interpretations onto others. Jesus had a problem with that. Like yeast in bread, a little yeast (lies/error/false teaching) spreads and can do a whole lot of damage. Are all signs from God? Clearly Scripture teaches that the apostles did signs and wonders. God is still powerful just like He was back then: *"And by the hands of the apostles were many signs and wonders done among the people; and they were all with one accord in Solomon's porch" (Acts 5:12, ESV).* He can do anything.

However, Scripture also contains warnings about being duped and following fake signs and wonders: *"The coming of the lawless one is according to the working of Satan, with all power, signs, and lying wonders, and with all unrighteous deception among those who perish, because they did not receive the love of the truth, that they might be saved. And for this reason God will send them strong delusion, that they should believe the lie, that they all may be condemned who did not believe the truth but had pleasure in unrighteousness" (2 Thessalonians 2:9-12, NKJV).* "If there arises among you a prophet or a dreamer of dreams, and he gives you a sign or a wonder, and the sign or the wonder comes to pass, of which he spoke to you, saying, 'Let us go after other gods'—which you have not known—'and let us serve them,' you shall not listen to the words of that prophet or that dreamer of dreams, for the **Lord your God is testing you to know whether you love the Lord your God with all your heart and with all your soul.** *You shall walk after the Lord your God and fear Him, and keep His commandments and obey His voice; you shall serve Him and hold fast to Him." (Deuteronomy 13:1-4, KJV)*

Interestingly, there are no records of feathers falling on the apostles in the Bible, though this is an occurrence happening in occultic religions and practices. According to a New Age ministry called "Krysalis Training Academy", which supports the Dalai Lama, psychic practices, reiki, New Age spiritual healing, hypnotherapy, eastern meditation, shamanism, wicca, mysticism and more - feathers are indeed a sign:

"Angels often send us little reminders of their presence as angel feathers, which are small white feathers. These seem to appear from nowhere when we are down and in need of comfort. I remember sitting in a café, watching the rain falling on the pavement outside and feeling blue. Suddenly, a small white feather floated down in front of me and landed on my table. I smiled, knowing the angels were around me, with their comforting presence".

Are these angel feathers falling from God or not? As we see here, feathers do appear as signs from other spirits of the occult.

God never asks us to "check our brains at the door". What these teachers are doing is a clever manipulation tactic: attempting to disarm and brainwash the minds of people by getting them to lay aside their brain power, discernment and intellect, and sadly, they are successful at this. This is called mind-control, of course, and getting people to doubt their discernment. Also, the Holy Spirit does work with our minds (Romans 12:2), for the Scriptures even say that He "re-minds" us of things: *"But the Comforter, who is the Holy Spirit, whom the Father will send in my name, he shall teach you all things, and bring all things to your remembrance, whatsoever I have said unto you."* (John 14:26, ESV) To remember is to *use the mind*. Don't think for a minute that God does not want you to use your brain, mind or God-given intellect and discernment (1 John 4:1). Christianity is an intelligent religion, not a blind faith.

CHRISTIAN MYSTICISM

Christian mysticism is a difficult term to define. It is often thought of as the practice of the experiential knowledge of God. The term can also apply to the mystery of the Eucharist in Roman Catholicism as well as so-called hidden meanings of Scripture, such as in Gnosticism. Gnostics believed they were an elite group that obtained a secret, inner and mystical knowledge.

The Bible does not have hidden meanings, nor do the elements of communion become Christ's literal body and blood. Although it is true that Christians experience God, Christian mysticism tends to elevate experiential knowledge and revel in the mysterious, focusing on mysticism for spiritual growth. Biblical Christianity focuses on knowing God through His Word (the Bible) and communion with the Holy Spirit through prayer. Mysticism tends to be an individual, subjective practice whereas Biblical Christianity is both an individual relationship with God and one that is necessarily lived out in community. Mysticism can be found in many religions. Often it involves asceticism of some type and seeks union with God. It is certainly right to want to draw close to God, but mystical union with God is different from the type of intimacy with God to which Christians are called. Mysticism tends to seek out the experience and is sometimes seen as secretive or elitist. Christians are aware of and engaged in spiritual realities (Ephesians 1:3; 6:10–19) and Biblical Christianity involves spiritual experience, but intimacy with God is intended for all Christians and is not veiled by any sort of mysterious practice. Drawing near to God is nothing mysterious or elitist but involves things like regular prayer, studying God's Word, worshipping God, and fellowshipping with other believers. Our efforts pale in comparison to the work God Himself does in us. In fact, our efforts are more a response to His work than they are something that originates in us.

The Charismatic movement, with its emphasis on dreams and visions, feelings and experiences, and new revelation, is one form of Christian mysticism. Because we have God's completed Word, we are not to seek after dreams and visions or extra revelation from God. While it is possible for God to reveal Himself in dreams and visions today, we should beware the subjective nature of feelings and spiritual impressions. The founders and promoters of many of the cults, make claim to *special revelation* from God upon which their system is built.

It is vital to remember that anything a Christian experiences must line up with the truth of the Bible. God will not contradict Himself. He is not the author of confusion (1 Corinthians 14:33). God is certainly beyond our full comprehension, and there is much that is mysterious about Him. But He has revealed Himself to us. Rather than seek out mystical experiences, we should involve ourselves in the things God has revealed to us (Deuteronomy 29:29). Ephesians 1:3–14 (ESV), talks about spiritual blessings in Christ. In part, that passage says, *"[God] made known to us the mystery of his will according to his good pleasure, which he purposed in Christ, to be put into effect when the times reach their fulfillment—to bring unity to all things in heaven and on earth under Christ" (v. 9–10)*. God has revealed mystery and calls us to faithfully walk in His ways as He completes His plan (John 15:1–17; Philippians 3:20–21; 2 Corinthians 5:16–21). Forms of mysticism was voiced in the teachings of Francis de Sales, Thomas à Kempis, Madam Guyon, Archbishop Fènelon, and Upham. Montanus advanced these conceptions as early as the second century.

YOGA

Focusing on a series of stretching exercises, breathing practices, and meditation to reach a state of peace and harmony, this physical discipline is merely a means to an end. It is a spiritual exercise and the spiritual awakening is really the serpent power (Kundalini), an energy that when released streams up the spine, where tremors, spasms and sometimes violent shaking and twisting are experienced. Yoga was introduced by Hindu's Lord Krishna in the Baghavad Gita as the sure way to Hindu heaven. In one of the most authoritative Hatha Yoga texts, the fifteenth-century HathaYoga Pradipika, Svatmarama lists Lord Shiva, (one of Hinduism's most feared Hindu deities, called "The Destroyer") as the first Hatha Yoga teacher. Shiva is addressed as Yogeshzuara, or Lord of Yoga. There are many types of Yoga. Besides the Ashtanga Yoga of Patanjali, - the most famous forms of Yoga are those described in the Bhavagad Gita, the Hindus sacred Scriptures. The best-known part of the epic Mahabharata, the Gita mentions Karma, Jnana, and Bhakti Yoga. These are not different types of Yoga but are different applications of Yoga to daily life. Since Yoga means to unite they are all part of the whole. In addition to these, there is Raja, Tantra, and Integral Yoga.

The Yoga positions are designed to reach the state of Samadhi, or a state of union with self as God. Hatha Yoga in its postures bring the subtle body into a specific alignment with the physical which will alter the consciousness of the participant. In other words, one is practicing one of the essential elements of Hinduism when doing their Hatha Yoga exercises; whether they are aware of it or not. Hatha

Yoga plays an important part in the development of the human being... the body working in harmony with the mind, to bring the seeker into closer contact with the Higher Self. Pranayama is the breathing process; by inhalation, exhalation one absorbs vital energy. Some claim by controlling Prana (life force), one can control all the forces of the universe, gravity (this why some claim to levitate), magnetism, electricity and their own nerve currents.

John Weldon and Clifford Wilson wrote in *Occult Shock and Psychic Forces* that Yoga is really pure occultism. Hans-Urich Rieker, in his book The Yoga of Light, also warns that misunderstanding the true nature of Yoga can mean "death or insanity." Also a little known fact is that virtually every major guru in India has issued warnings similar to these; i.e., *deep breathing techniques such as the ones taught in Yoga are a time-honored method for entering altered states of consciousness and for developing so-called psychic power.*

Yoga is one of the basic means of reaching this altered state of consciousness. And the altered state is the doorway to the occult. Sir John Eccles, Nobel Prize Winner for his research on the brain, said the brain is "a machine that a ghost can operate." In a normal state of consciousness one's own spirit ticks off the neurons in his brain and operates his body. We are spirits connected with a body. But in an altered state, reached under drugs, Yoga, hypnosis, visualization, this passive but alert state, the connection between the spirit and the brain, is loosened. That allows another spirit to interpose itself, to begin to tick off the neurons in the brain, and create an entire universe of illusion. You've then opened yourself up to the spiritual realm which God forbids for us to enter. It's called sorcery. Those encouraged to use meditation, Yoga, visualization, chakra energizing, or spirit guides could certainly be taken advantage of by the enemy.

Unbeknown to many people, they are literally teaching themselves how to be demonized, asking guiding spirits to help teach and relieve them of their stress, all in the name of stress reduction and developing one's full potential. The fact is, the person who is practicing Yoga, they are taught that the Asana's, are to be able to release themselves from the trappings of reincarnation by working off their karma.

Yoga is to help one neutralize their karma and find a way off the cycle of rebirth (reincarnation). How can these spiritual exercises be sanitized for Christian use and for what reason would it be used? To relax? The Bible teaches that God will *"keep him in perfect peace, whose mind is stayed on You, because he trusts in You." (Isa. 26:3, NKJV)* One cannot make an excuse that they want to use it to experience peace and or the divine.

The poses that they so diligently practice in their stretching are named after Hindu Gods, and what one is actually doing, is calling on them. In that worshipful pose, they are bowing and for all intents and purposes worshipping THAT God. Our God says *"You shall have no other Gods before me. You shall not make for yourself an idol in the form of anything in heaven above or on the earth beneath or in the waters below. You shall not bow down to them or worship them; for I, the Lord your God, am a jealous God." (Exodus 20, 3-5, NRSV)*

As Christians who are in relationship with the God who created the universe, we should not be among those who exchanged the truth of God for a lie, and worship and serve created things rather than the Creator (Romans 1:25). While many Christians rationalize the exercises as neutral, they only need to ask a professional Yoga instructor what it is really about to find that it is in fact "religious". As a Christian, we need to ask ourselves would Jesus or the apostles be doing Yoga? If not, why not? Would they promote another religions' way to be united with different gods? According to the Bible, Yoga is an idolatrous practice which leads one away from the one true God and into the spiritual realm of false gods and demonic spirits, and there are consequences. If we sin ignorantly God understands, He is merciful, giving us grace on the one hand, but not to continue after we receive knowledge of the truth. This does not diminish the fact that there are still consequences. On the other hand, He cares of our sin, not willing to leave us to our deception. *"My people are destroyed from lack of knowledge." (Hosea 4:6, ESV)* In Hosea's time, people had a lack of knowledge concerning God. As a result, they turned to other gods, and their idolatrous practices became a snare to them and a delusion. They became the prey of false gods-even while thinking that their lifestyle was pleasing to the true God.

There is absolutely no problem in stretching exercises in and of themselves. What would be wrong is taking Yoga positions assuming they are stretching exercises and non-religious, when in fact they are worshipful poses to Hindu gods. No one can deny that stretching helps the blood flow and breathing in oxygen helps our overall health. There are numerous other ways unattached to a religion that can accomplish this. There are numerous exercise programs that incorporate stretching that in no way relates to Yoga (and its' worldview) that one can substitute. Religious syncretism is probably the most dangerous we can involve ourselves in because we can rationalize its purpose. From the Hindu viewpoint nothing is merely physical, because in Hinduism the physical is merely maya, an illusion, so when you practice Yoga it is not a physical exercise for the body but a spiritual exercise. All these can be pursued in other ways than having it attached to a religion that teaches you to discover you are god. Essentially one cannot practice a portion of Hinduism and continue to walk with the true Christ who is not a Hindu Guru.

HOROSCOPES/ASTROLOGY

The word "horoscope" which comes from the Greek and means, "watcher of the hour" was first coined in an ancient, declining Greece that began to tolerate astrology after long resisting it. Horoscopes, as innocuous as they may appear, are not just products of the imagination. The authors of these columns are usually astrologers; some are psychics. Astrologers have purposely studied what they believe to be the meanings of the planets, the zodiac signs, and other astrological data. Along with this information, they consider the present positions of planets (and the sun and moon), and how they interact with the sun signs of Aries, Taurus, Gemini, etc., in order to give horoscope advice. Since the moon changes signs every 2.5 days, its position is a key element in the forecasting.

Astrological philosophy is based on the occult worldview that asserts "as above, so below." According to this view, everything in the universe is one and is connected; therefore, the patterns of the planets reflect our lives on earth.

Astrology is the "interpretation" of an assumed influence the stars (and planets) exert on human destiny. This is a false belief. The royal astrologers of the Babylonian court were put to shame by God's prophet Daniel (Daniel 1:20) and were powerless to interpret the king's dream (Daniel 2:27). God specifies astrologers as among those who will be burned as stubble in God's judgment (Isaiah 47:13-14). Astrology as a form of divination is expressly forbidden in Scripture (Deuteronomy 18:10-14). God forbade the children of Israel to worship or serve the "host of heaven" (Deuteronomy 4:19). Several times in their history, however, Israel fell into that very sin (2 Kings 17:16 is one example). Their worship of the stars brought God's judgment each time.

The stars should awaken wonder at God's power, wisdom, and infinitude. We should use the stars to keep track of time and place and to remind us of God's faithful, covenant-keeping nature. All the while, we acknowledge the Creator of the heavens. Our wisdom comes from God, not the stars (James 1:5). The Word of God, the Bible, is our guide through life (Psalm 119:105).

The very roots of astrology are in ancient paganism and worship of the planets as gods, making astrology a true form of *"fellowship with the unfruitful works of darkness "* *(Ephesians 5:11, KJV)*. Most astrologers are involved in other forms of occultism and New Age practices such as tarot cards, numerology, belief in reincarnation, having spirit guides, Eastern meditation practices, and so forth. Thus, reading horoscopes (as well as consulting an astrologer) is to be receptive to something coming from this kind of spiritual worldview.

Being an occult art, astrology is connected to the paranormal powers of the occult. Take the Word of God with trembling and fear. God will not compromise with sin and the divination of the future by use of astrology or horoscopes makes Him righteously angry. Don't go there. Not even for curiosity, *"for whoever does these things is an abomination to the Lord" (Deuteronomy 18:12, NKJV) for "the Lord your God has not allowed you to do this" (Deuteronomy 18:14, NKJV)*.

PSYCHICS

A *Psychic* is a person with the ability of ESP (Extra-Sensory-Perception). The word 'Psychic' originates from the Greek word 'psychikos' (Pertaining to the Soul) and refers to the 'psyche' (the human mind). When a psychic gives a *psychic reading* or a consultation this would include intuitively perceiving information about the sitter using *clairvoyance* (seership) and *telepathy* (mind to mind communication). In some cases, this can include information that is already in your mind but also extraordinary information about your situation. Many people visit a psychic because they want to know about the future – a demonic gift known as *precognition*.

Channeling is a method of trying to communicate with the spirit world that has existed since antiquity. Most modern channelers learn the art through the practice of Eastern meditation. This mildly altered state of consciousness enables the channeler to psychically perceive spirit messages. These manifest themselves as a "thought voice," which is perceived in the stillness of the medium's mind. Experienced mediums can enter into a trance state whereby the spirit entity takes direct control over the medium's voice, speaking through it in an accent quite distinct from the medium's normal mode of speech.

It is claimed that the telepathic communications come from highly evolved spirit beings existing in the normally invisible realms of the spirit dimension. Sometimes the medium will have a vision in which he or she sees the spirit in a visible form, manifested in the imagination faculties of the medium's consciousness. The spirit guides are said to sometimes wear white robes and often radiate brilliant, golden-white light. Channelers claim that the messages received represent divine wisdom and truth, and have beneficial value for mankind. It is undeniable that psychics sometimes know things that should be impossible for them to know. Where do they get this information? The answer is from Satan and his demons. *"And no wonder, for Satan himself masquerades as an angel of light. It is not surprising, then, if his servants masquerade as servants of righteousness. Their end will be what their actions deserve."* (2 Corinthians 11:14-15, NIV)

Spiritists and mediums were common among the pagan peoples of the Bible lands. God warned the children of Israel against becoming involved in these practices just prior to their entry into the Promised Land of Canaan. *"When you enter the land the Lord your God is giving you, do not learn to imitate the detestable ways of the nations there. Let no one be found among you who sacrifices his son or daughter in the fire, who practices divination or sorcery, interprets omens, engages in witchcraft, or casts spells, or who is a medium or spiritist or who consults the dead. Anyone who does these things is detestable to the Lord."* (Deuteronomy 18:9-12, NIV)

Among the Israelites, the penalty for anyone practicing spiritism was death. *"A man or woman who is a medium or a spiritist among you must be put to death."* (Leviticus 20:27, NIV)

Satan pretends to be kind and helpful. He tries to appear as something good. Satan and his demons will give psychic information about a person in order to get that person hooked into spiritism, something that God forbids. It appears innocent at first, but soon people can find themselves addicted to psychics and unwittingly allow Satan to control and destroy their lives.

PALM READING

Palmistry (palm reading) is known by the Greek word, chiromancy, which is defined as foretelling the future through the study of the palm. The practice of palmistry was practiced as far back as 5000 years ago, and is traced back to Indian or Hindu roots. It then spread to China, Greece, Egypt, Persia, and Tibet as well as to other parts of Europe. Palm reading, also known as "palmistry" or "chiromancy," has its roots in Greek mythology. *Chiromancy*, from the Greek *kheiro*, meaning "hand," and *mantia*, meaning "divination," essentially means "divination from the palm of the hand." Practitioners believe they can interpret one's character, fortunes, and possible future events by "reading" the lines, marks, and bumps on the palm of a person's hand.

Palm reading, also known as palmistry and chiromancy, is the attempt to read the lines in a person's palm and thereby determine such things as how smart the person is, how long he will live, his personality traits, habits, and even his fortune. The practice occurs all over the world and different cultures contradict other cultures when it comes to palm reading. Proponents maintain that the various lines on the palm deal with the heart, life, fate, and more.

There is absolutely no evidence that palm reading works. Generally, those who seek knowledge through the reading of their palms are already open to vague interpretations of the palm readers. When a person opens himself up to such false things, he is opening himself up to deception. Some palm readers are good at speaking in generalities and reading the emotional and body language cues from a subject in order to determine what to say thereby draw the person in and either get money or keep them coming back. Undoubtedly, however, there are those who believe in palm reading and are not intending to deceive but are being used by the spiritual realm to deceive others.

Nevertheless, palm reading is a form of divination and is condemned in Scripture. Divination: "The art of determining the future or ascertaining the divine will. Practiced widely throughout the ancient Near East, divination involved the observation and interpretation of natural phenomena or of phenomena deliberately caused by the person or persons interpreting these omens."

Divination was also condemned by the prophets (Isaiah 44:25; Jeremiah 27:9; 29:8; Ezekiel 13:9). Such occult practices were very common among the pagan nations of the ancient world. And it was, in part, because of these detestable practices that God threw out the people of Canaan and replaced them with the Israelites (Deuteronomy 18:12, 14).

Christians can be confident in the knowledge that our sovereign God is in control of our unseen future. The answers we seek are not in our hands but in God's. Anyone who is anxious about the future need only hear the words of our Lord: *"Do not worry about your life, what you will eat or drink; or about your body, what you will wear . . . for the pagans run after all these things, and your heavenly Father knows that you need them. But seek first His kingdom and His righteousness, and all these things will be given to you as well. Therefore do not worry about tomorrow, for tomorrow will worry about itself." (Matthew 6:25, 32–34, NIV)*

ESSENTIAL OILS

Since the beginning of time, people have been using oils for medicinal and spiritual purposes. In fact, Ancient Egypt is known for its mystical wisdom in oils. This is nothing new. There is nothing good or evil about oil. It is an object. It is natural, just like cannabis or crystals. The problem is always in HOW men try to use it.

There has been a sudden and alarming trend of Christian women promoting essential oils for medicinal purposes. Natural remedies are great. If chicken soup can make you better, cook it, eat it, enjoy it! But some of these companies have very serious New Age and occult connections.

Gary Young is the founder of Young Living oils and he is a "professing" Christian. You can find him discussing the twelve oils of Scripture at a website called BiospiritualEnergyHealing.com. In this article, Young talks about the "Third Eye" being opened by the use of essential oils. This is also referred to by the Pineal Gland. This is not a Christian belief. It isn't even a scientific belief. It is **only** a pagan belief.

"Many people have said that we communicate to our Father through the pineal gland. I have not found documentation on that, so I don't know that it is a correct statement, but I do believe when you have a spiritual experience you get this warm, burning, fuzzy feeling in your bosom. The chemical that creates that warm fuzzy feeling in your bosom is secreted from the pineal gland, and that may be the reason we are told by some scientists that the pineal gland is responsible for that communication. Very special" (Young).

This is New Age and demonic. He says this in the section called "Increasing Spiritual Communication." Well, if he was actually communicating with the God of the Bible, because this oil opened his third eye, then why is he spouting demonic lies and not Biblical truth?

If you go to Young Living's website you can easily find the page dedicated to their oil blends. This is where we can easily see the truth behind this company. To really understand where we are going, you need to understand what this type of witchcraft is. I am sure you have all heard the word "potion" before. The word for sorcery in Greek is *Pharmakeia* (Strongs Greek 5331). These words refer to medicines or drugs that are combined together to accomplish a physical or spiritual intention. It is a potion. This is exactly how witches have been using oils, way before Christians got involved. And this is exactly how Young Living is openly marketing their oils.

Young Living's "oil blends" are blatant potions. This is so satanic. In fact, they even use the phrase "law of attraction" which is the whole basis for the occult book *The Secret*. The Berean Call ministry says, "*The Secret* is not a secret at all, but recycled Hinduism, Shamanism, and New Age folly. One of many huge lies is its claim: "You create your own reality with your mind." This was the serpent's false promise to Eve–the promise of godhood" (The Secret Seduction) An OIL can enhance visualization, and spiritual dreams? This is not a medicine. This is a potion. This is occult.

"Trauma Live" says it is:

"a calming, grounding blend of therapeutic-grade essential oils formulated to help release buried emotional trauma resulting from accidents, neglect, the death of a loved one, assault, or abuse. Left unchecked, emotionally draining episodes may be at the root of fatigue, anger, and restlessness."

"Inspiration" helps you connect spiritually, just like pagans did!—

"Inspiration™ includes oils traditionally used by the native peoples of Arabia, India, and North America for enhancing spirituality, prayer, meditation, and inner awareness. It creates an aromatic sanctuary for those seeking quiet meditation and spirituality."

Another oil that combines paganism with pseudo science —

*"Australian Blue™ is a powerful, aromatic essence that unites **ancient aboriginal wisdom** with today's scientific knowledge about essential oils to uplift and inspire the mind and heart. This exotic essential oil blend has sweet, earthy undertones responsible for its calming and stabilizing effects."*

And "Aroma Life" helps your life force, or vital energy (chakra) —

"Aroma Life™ combines the harmonizing effects of ylang ylang with known powerhouses cypress, helichrysum, and marjoram. Pulsing with life, this vibrant blend energizes your life force. It is best applied over heart energy – front and/or back."

Your " life force" is a New Age occult word for "psychic energy". Another word for this is Chi or Prana. Hindus believe in this. It is totally New Age. If you click on the "Balance" page you will see them discuss this life force a little more:

"The world moves at a blistering pace. Rediscover tranquility when you slow down and seek out the small moments of bliss that keep spiritual and emotional wellness in balance.

Tap into your own vital life energy with pure essential oils and blends formulated for their ability to promote inner peace and emotional well-being. Our Balance products can guide you to your spiritual and emotional center, helping you live fully in the present moment."

Here is the description for the oil called "Friends"—

A social circle, comprised of both friends and acquaintances, is vital to our well-being. It is valuable to expand and improve your friend base as you pursue a life in Oola.

The INFUSED Friends™ Inspired by Oola essential oil blend has been specially formulated to bring harmonic balance to the energy centers of the body, which encourages feelings of self-worth, empowerment, confidence, and awareness.

Friends affirmation: I am blessed with empowering, healthy relationships.

Part of the INFUSED 7 kit which includes the Inspired by Oola® essential oil blends: Faith™, Fitness™, Finance™, Friends™, Family™, Field™, and Fun™

"Sensation" is for sex, "Slique" is for thinness, "Abundance" is for money, "Release" helps you deal with repressed anger, "Present Time" helps you move on from the past, "Calming" helps your kids behave, "Motivation" helps you get things accomplished, "Longevity" helps you look younger, "Common Sense" helps you make good decisions, and "Valor" helps support your energy alignment in your body, or your Chi. This is insane. I have Christian friends that want me to come to their house on a Saturday for an oil party where they will try to persuade me to spend HUNDREDS of dollars on these oils. But who doesn't want happiness, money, beauty, and health? Who doesn't want to deal with anger, with just a simple dab of oil? It is so seductive! And it smells good!

In fact, if you go to a pagan oil dealer you will find oil blends for sale that have the same claims that Young Living and DoTerra have. Check out the Organic Witch.

"Nothin' Says Lovin' Like Somethin' from the Coven!"

I personally, would choose to throw away all oil blends that promise me money, visualization, life energy, etc. The list goes on. That is witchcraft and I will have nothing to do with witchcraft under my roof. The same way I would not have a satanic album in my CD collection (a compact disc is not evil, but the music is). The same way I won't have a Ouija board in my house (a cardboard game is not evil, but divination is).

"You must not do as they do in Egypt, where you used to live, and you must not do as they do in the land of Canaan, where I am bringing you. Do not follow their practices." (Leviticus 18:22, NIV)

KARMA

Karma is a theological concept found in the New Age, Buddhist, Sikh, Hindu and Jain religions. It is the idea that how you live your life will determine the quality of life you will have after reincarnation. If you are unselfish, kind, and holy during this lifetime, you will be rewarded by being reincarnated (reborn into a new earthly body) into a pleasant life. However, if you live a life of selfishness and evil, you will be reincarnated into a less-than-pleasant lifestyle. In other words, you reap in the next life what you sow in this one. Karma is based on the theological belief in reincarnation. The Bible rejects the idea of reincarnation; therefore, it does not support the idea of karma.

What's more, karma says all of us will live again, to either a better or worse life based on what we do today. The Bible, however, says that we can only live if we believe in the Son of God (see Romans 6:23; John 3:16-17). Our actions can't win a better afterlife for us – only the blood of the Jesus can.

The Bible talks a lot about reaping and sowing. Job 4:8 (NIV) says, *"As I have observed, those who plow evil and those who sow trouble reap it."* Psalm 126:5 (NIV) says, *"Those who sow in tears will reap with songs of joy."* Luke 12:24 (NIV) says, *"Consider the ravens: They do not sow or reap, they have no storeroom or barn; yet God feeds them. And how much more valuable you are than birds!"* In each of these instances, as well as all the other references to reaping and sowing, the act of receiving the rewards of your actions takes place in this life, not in some future life. It is a present-day activity, and the references make it clear that the fruit you reap will be commensurate with the actions you have performed. In addition, the sowing you perform in this life will affect your reward or punishment in the afterlife.

This afterlife is not a rebirth or a reincarnation into another body here on earth. It is either eternal suffering in hell (Matthew 25:46) or eternal life in heaven with Jesus, who died so that we might live eternally with Him. This should be the focus of our life on earth. The apostle Paul wrote in Galatians 6:8-9 (NIV), *"The one who sows to please his sinful nature, from that nature will reap destruction; the one who sows to please the Spirit, from the Spirit will reap eternal life. Let us not become weary in doing good, for at the proper time we will reap a harvest if we do not give up."*

It is only through Jesus' sacrifice that our good deeds will produce any real good (Philippians 2:13). Galatians 6:8-9 (NIV) explains that *"whoever sows to please the Spirit, from the Spirit will reap eternal life."* 1 Corinthians 9:24-25 (NIV) says that in this life, we can run the race so as to win an imperishable crown in the next. We cannot do this through our own effort. Karma says that our good can outweigh our bad. The Bible says our good works are like filthy rags (Isaiah 64:6), but Jesus' works make us a new creation, reconciled to God, unstained by our own sin (2 Corinthians 5:17-20).

REINCARNATION

Reincarnation is the philosophical or religious concept that an aspect of a living being starts a new life in a different physical body or form after each biological death. It is also called rebirth or transmigration, and is a part of the Saṃsāra doctrine of cyclic existence. It is a central tenet of all major Indian religions, namely Buddhism, Hinduism, Jainism, and Sikhism. The idea of reincarnation is found in many ancient cultures, and a belief in rebirth/metempsychosis was held by Greek historic figures, such as Pythagoras, Socrates, and Plato. It is also a common belief of various ancient and modern religions such as Spiritism, Theosophy, and Eckankar and is found as well in many tribal societies around the world, in places such as Australia, East Asia, Siberia, and South America.

The whole thrust of the Bible opposes reincarnation. It shows that man is the special creation of God, created in God's image with both a material body and an immaterial soul and spirit. He is presented as distinct and unique from all other creatures—angels and the animal kingdom alike. The Bible teaches that at death, while man's body is mortal, decays and returns to dust, his soul and spirit continue on either in a place of torments for those who reject Christ or in paradise (heaven) in God's presence for those who have trusted in the Savior. Both categories of people will be resurrected, one to eternal judgment and the other to eternal life with a glorified body (John 5:25-29). The emphatic statement of the Bible, as will be pointed out below, is that *"it is appointed unto men once to die and after that the judgment"* (Heb. 9:27, NKJV). This statement and the concept that mankind's creation in God's image is unique from the animals and even angels stand totally opposed to the idea of reincarnation—dying and coming back as another person or in the form of an animal or insect. The claim of some that they have information of past history is nothing more than some kind of encounter with demonic powers who have been present throughout history.

Those that believe in reincarnation also like to use the verse found in John 3:3 (NKJV) to prove that there is reincarnation in the Bible. The verse states, *"In reply Jesus declared, 'I tell you the truth, no one can see the kingdom of God unless he is born again.'"* This is perhaps the most frequently quoted verse that is used to support reincarnation in the Bible. However, the verse is taken out of context, and just two verses later, Jesus explains what He means by "born again." It says, *"Jesus answered, 'I tell you the truth, no one can enter the kingdom of God unless he is born of water and the Spirit'"* (John 3:5, NKJV). Here one sees that Jesus was clearly talking about a spiritual rebirth, not a physical one.

Finally, the most telling verse against reincarnation in the Bible is found in Hebrews 9:27 (NIV) where it states, *"Just as man is destined to die once, and after that to face judgment."* This makes it clear that humanity only dies once and is then judged on the life he has lived. One is not born again in an endless cycle of death and rebirth, and its attendant opportunity to improve one's karma (karma being an associated doctrine of reincarnation that means if one leads a good life one will be reincarnated into a better situation in the next life). Death awaits all of us because all of us are sinners, and that Jesus' sacrificial death on the cross has freed us from this death and has brought eternal life in heaven to all who believe.

CHRIST CONSCIOUSNESS

The term *Christ consciousness* has gained popularity in recent years as celebrities and public figures claim that they have "found truth" in this form of spirituality. Those championing this idea sometimes call themselves Christians; however, their definition of the word *Christian* is far different from the Biblical meaning. The name of the Lord Jesus Christ is used as a means of normalizing a religion which is nothing more than rebranded Eastern mysticism.

The Center for Christ Consciousness website defines *Christ consciousness* as "the highest state of intellectual development and emotional maturity." They go on to claim that "Jesus achieved this [higher state of being] in his human life, and was given this term [Christ] before his name as the recognition of his achievement of this spiritual status. This path is open to anyone regardless of their religious tradition if and when he or she is open to become a living vessel of love and truth on the planet and actively strives to attain it." Another site defines it this way: "Christ consciousness is the state of awareness of our true nature, our higher self, and our birthright as children of God." It does not take much research to uncover the ancient roots of this idea. It is the same man-centered philosophy that is behind most religions.

So-called "Christ consciousness" has been known by various names in history, such as Jainism, Buddhism, Hinduism, and most Eastern mystical religions. More recently, Deepak Chopra has popularized the "Christianized" version of this same pseudo-spirituality. The danger in this latest version of mysticism is the use of Bible verses and Christian terms, which can easily lead astray those who don't check the Scriptures for themselves.

The basic premise of mysticism is that man can, within himself, transcend physical existence and experience his own goodness as being "one" with the universe, being a god, or existing on whatever higher plane he chooses to believe in. The name of Jesus is merely used as a prop in this latest version of the same idea. Jesus is seen as the "leader" in showing us how to exalt our own inner goodness and, in doing so, make ourselves right with whatever deity we choose to acknowledge. Christ consciousness groups claim that Jesus earned the title "Christ" by perfectly channeling the divine consciousness we can all attain, and they attempt to attribute this philosophy to the Lord Jesus. Those championing this ideology are merely using the name of Jesus as a means of worshiping themselves. They desire to find absolution without repentance, confession of sin, or acknowledging Jesus' substitutionary death and resurrection (1 Corinthians 15:3–4).

Christ consciousness claims a belief in Jesus Christ, but it actually promotes faith in one's own ability to make oneself pleasing to God through attitude changes and mystical experiences. Galatians 2:16 (ESV) states that *"a person is not justified by the works of the law, but by faith in Jesus Christ . . . that we may be justified by faith in Christ and not by the works of the law, because by the works of the law no one will be justified."* Faith in Christ does not mean we strive to be like Him in our own strength. He did not present Himself as a great moral teacher. He was crucified because He claimed to be the "only begotten Son of God" (John 1: 14, 18; 3:15–18; 1 John 4:9). Becoming *"conformed to the image of Christ"* (Romans 8:29, ESV) comes through the power of the Holy Spirit, given to those who repent and receive Jesus as Savior and Lord (John 1:12; Mark 6:12; 2 Corinthians 5:5).

REIKI

Reiki can be defined as a non-physical healing energy made up of **life force energy** that is guided by the Higher Intelligence, or spiritually guided life force energy. Reiki is a Japanese technique for stress reduction and relaxation that also promotes healing. It is administered by "laying on hands" and is based on the idea that an unseen "life force energy" flows through us and is what causes us to be alive. If one's "life force energy" is low, then we are more likely to get sick or feel stress, and if it is high, we are more capable of being happy and healthy.

The word Reiki is made of two Japanese words - *Rei* which means "God's Wisdom or the Higher Power" and *Ki* which is "life force energy". So Reiki is actually "spiritually guided life force energy.

A treatment feels like a wonderful glowing radiance that flows through and around you. Reiki treats the whole person including body, emotions, mind and spirit creating many beneficial effects that include relaxation and feelings of peace, security and wellbeing. Many have reported miraculous results.

An increasing number of Christian organizations and Churches are embracing Reiki just as they are embracing other mystical practices such as **contemplative prayer**. The reason for this level of acceptance is easy to understand. Most people, many Christians included, believe if something is spiritually positive then it is of God.

Reiki instructors function in a manner indistinguishable from psychic healers who utilize spirit guides. Reiki is again, described as "the art and science of taping, activating and directing natural universal energy" and "with this technique, a higher frequency of natural energy passes from the hands of the therapist to those whom he touches. If a physical healing *does* occur through Reiki, let the practitioner and the client *beware*. Why *beware* of such a thing? Because a very sinister trade-off has transpired! Yes a real physical healing *may* occur through the practice of Reiki, but so too, a very deeply rooted form of spiritual deception will take place on a much deeper level - within the individuals very being.

In off-base Christian groups and Cults, the *occult-oriented* laying on of hands often times produces manifestations, but they are either psychosomatic in origin, purely demonic, or both. Reiki can and does at times, produce manifestations, but they are clearly not from the God of the Bible. God never sanctions or endorses occult practices. Rather, He condemns every form of them. His blanket condemnation of engaging in such practices is clearly revealed in His Word (Deuteronomy 18:9-14).

Many individuals who delve into New Age and occult practices have suffered the consequences of spiritual oppression, occult bondage, psychological delusion, insanity, irreversible mental and physical damage, insanity, suicidal tendencies, possession states, moral degradation, sexual perversion, fatal accidents, and more.

HOLISTIC MEDICINE

Some Christians, if they knew more about the religious connections of alternative medicine, wouldn't want to participate. There's also evidence that practicing something connected with religion can actually change people's beliefs. Christians, in particular, tend to think a person's intent determines whether something is religious. They don't realize that active participation can actually change someone's intent. Over time, people who start off attracted to an alternative practice because there's a perceived health benefit start to embrace the religious ideas underneath these practices.

The holistic belief is that health has more than just a physical component and is, in fact, also related to the mental, emotional, social and spiritual state of the individual. To be healthy, all facets of a person must be addressed, and all must be treated for there to be true health. According to the American Holistic Health Association, "Ancient healing traditions, as far back as 5,000 years ago in India and China, stressed living a healthy way of life in harmony with nature.

Alternative methods of therapy included under the umbrella of holistic medicine include, but are not limited to, nutrition, herbal medicine, spinal manipulation, body work medicine, energy medicine, spiritual attunement, relaxation training and stress management, biofeedback and acupuncture.

Many holistic health advocates recommend techniques for spiritual wellness that may ultimately be in conflict with Scripture and even become open doors for demonic activity. Because of its roots in ancient Eastern cultures, holistic medicine often advocates transcendental meditation, a technique for emptying the mind and becoming "one with the universe." It encourages participants to seek the answers to life's difficult questions within their own conscience instead of in the Word of God. It also leaves one open to deception from God's enemy, who searches for victims that he can turn away from God (1 Peter 5:8). For the Christian, meditation should center on the Word of God, His attributes, and the beauty of Jesus Christ, the Great Physician.

Spirituality is an important concept within much of alternative medicine. Practitioners can be devout Christians or they can believe in worldviews that are radically different from a Biblically based worldview. Sometimes the same terms are used, but with meanings that are quite different. For example, prayer may be recommended by various therapists, but they may have completely different practices in mind. A few may actually involve occult practices. Some alternative medicine practitioners believe they cannot help their patients without first introducing them to one or another of the ancient Eastern or New Age faith systems. This leads to potential conflict for Christians. They may hear anecdotal stories from friends about shamanism easing arthritis pain without drugs, Therapeutic Touch increasing the speed of healing after wounds, or Reiki easing a chronic health condition. The stories are positive. Nothing is said about the spiritual side of the treatments or the demonic activity they invite. Satan is very clever and comes as an angel of light.

GRAVE SOAKING

Grave sucking, also known as grave soaking or mantle grabbing, is the act of lying across the physical grave of a deceased preacher or evangelist for the purpose of "pulling out" the power of the Holy Spirit, a power that was purportedly "trapped" within the body upon the person's death. The aberrant practice of grave sucking was initiated within the Charismatic movement and Word of Faith teachings, which are an amalgamation of orthodox Christianity and mysticism.

Grave sucking or mantle grabbing is based upon the idea that the spiritual calling of an individual who has died may be reclaimed and used by another person. The theory is that God uses the Holy Spirit to "anoint" certain believers with a specific purpose, such as healing or prophecy, but, when the person dies, God's work is thwarted. Thus, the Holy Spirit is "wasted," lying upon the bones and unable to continue the calling. Unrecovered anointing is apparently available to anyone who would physically come and claim it. This superstitious practice is blatantly unbiblical, spiritually dangerous, and tremendously misleading for uninformed believers.

2 Kings 13 gives us a story of a person who came back to life after touching the bones of Elisha. Some have no doubt that the power of God was still in his grave and/or that the miracle-working anointing of Elisha was still residually present on his bones. We have to remember that this is a strange, unique, mysterious story, and that it is dangerous to formulate a doctrine and/or practice based on one obscure passage. This is how cults have started. We need to compare Scripture with Scripture, and if there is an isolated, obscure

passage we encounter, then we should refrain from conjecture and not make a doctrine out of it until we can establish a clear Biblical pattern. Also, it must be noted that the person in this passage was raised from the dead. The Bible does not indicate that he received Elisha's anointing, mantle or became a prophet.

Furthermore, that may have been just one sovereign act of God to remind the Jews of their heritage and the unique prophetic calling Elijah handed down to Elisha. The spirit, power and anointing of these saints is no longer in the ground. The Bible teaches that when believers are absent from the body they are present with the Lord (2 Corinthians 5:8). This implies that our spirit leaves our body when we physically die. Hence, it is no longer on the earth and thus no longer in the grave.

In the Roman Catholic tradition we actually see the official practice of Mary worship and saint worship. Furthermore, it is common for a Roman Catholic to pray to one of the canonized departed saints. Whenever we go to a departed saint for something instead of directly to Jesus we violate Scriptures like 2 Timothy 2:5 and John 14:6, since we only have one designated mediator between God and man: Jesus Christ. Grave sucking comes perilously close to saint worship and, if not corrected, could also lead to communing (speaking) with departed saints. After all, if we can receive an anointing from the grave of a departed saint, who is to say we cannot receive advice and/or life altering visions from that same saint? Finally, this could eventually lead to necromancy, which is witchcraft and has to do with conjuring up the spirits of the dead. Scripture teaches this is wrong even if you are trying to contact a departed saint (1 Sam. 28).

PROPHETS/DIVINATION

Divination is a demonic counterfeit ability that the devil uses in order to foretell the future. It is the ability to access hidden knowledge or secrets pertaining to a person or a people or an event through demonic sources such as familiar spirits etc. The Greek word of divination comes from the root word PYTHON. The Spirit of Python counterfeits the Spirit of Prophecy. Divination is a form of witchcraft that possesses psychics, witchdoctors, false prophets, spiritual advisors, medicine men, New Age gurus, voodoo priests & priestess, mediums, etc. We are told in Deuteronomy 18:14 that we are not permitted to practice divination, sorcery or any witchcraft, for it is an abomination to God. The act of divining; a foretelling future events, or discovering things secret or obscure, by the aid of superior beings, or by other than human means.

Therefore when Jesus said that false prophets would perform signs and wonders, He did not lie, because false prophets use divination in order to foretell future events.

In Mathew 24:11(NKJV), Jesus Himself warned that *"MANY false prophets will rise up and (they will) deceive MANY"* and true to God's Word – today, many people claiming to be prophets of God have arisen all over the world and they have been performing various signs and wonders before masses of followers. However, such signs and wonders have been met with skepticism and the source of these signs and wonders is unknown as to whether such wonders come from God or from somewhere else. Godly prophecy edifies/builds the church, rebukes sin and draws humanity closer or back to God while divination does not. Majority of the people practicing divination use it for fame or to make money. All these people running seeking for personal prophecy and to know their future are all falling into hands of Satan's servants with the spirit of divination. After divining your life, the demonic servants lead you away from Jesus Christ. Every person telling you to pay to receive prophecy, future telling or to receive a miracle is Satan's servant. Stop seeking for personal prophecy and to know your future. Stop running to people with the spirit of divination. The entire future of a Christian is clearly revealed in the Bible. Believe. God says,

Leviticus 19:31(NKJV) "Regard not them that have familiar spirits, neither seek after wizards to be defiled by them: I am the LORD your God."

Leviticus 20:6 (NKJV) "And the soul that turns after such as have familiar spirits, and after wizards, to go a whoring after them, I will even set my face against that soul, and will cut him off from among his people."

When forbidden techniques are used, deception is gained. Today divination is rampant in the church. It is just as poisonous to the faith today as divination was to Israel's faith in the Old Testament. It is rebellion in that it involves refusing to stay within the boundaries God has set for our own good. Those who are thus deceived have put themselves into that horrible state because they did not receive the love of the truth (**2 Thessalonians 2:11, 12**). The truth is the Gospel of Jesus Christ. We need to purge divination from the church and replace it with Gospel preaching and Bible teaching.

FEMALE ANGELS

In the present fascination of our culture, previously referred to as *angelmania*, the common conception of angels is that of winged creatures and most times as female.

Some of the commonly held conceptions are not supported by the scriptural witness. There are no indications of angels appearing in female form. Nor is there explicit reference to them as winged, although Daniel 9:21 and Revelation 14:6 speak of them as flying. The cherubim and seraphim are represented as winged (Exod. 25:20; Isa. 6:2), as are the symbolic creatures of Ezekiel 1:6 (Rev. 4:8). However, we have no assurance that what is true of cherubim and seraphim is true of angels in general. Since there is no explicit reference indicating that angels as a whole are winged, we must regard this as at best an inference, but not a necessary inference, from the Biblical passages which describe them as flying.

Since all angles in the Bible were male in form, you should discern that female angels are satanic agents. However, this does not mean that all male-looking angels are from God. Masculine angels must be discerned on a case-by-case basis. God does not tell us why angels appear as male in the Bible and not female. Angels do not have gender since gender is a biological function, and angels are not biological. The only angels that are named in the Bible include Michael, Gabriel, and Lucifer, who are referred to in the masculine. Other angels are referred to in the masculine sense even though they are not named. The Greek word for "angel" in the New Testament is *angelos*, itself a masculine noun. A feminine form of this word does not exist.

The angels mentioned throughout the visions of Revelation are referred to with the pronouns "he" and "his."

When angels appeared, they were always dressed as human males (Genesis 18:2, 16; Ezekiel 9:2). No angel ever appears in Scripture dressed as a female. Some people point to Zechariah 5:9 as an example of female angels. That verse says, "Then I looked up—and there before me were two women, with the wind in their wings! They had wings like those of a stork, and they lifted up the basket between heaven and earth." The problem is that the "women" in this prophetic vision are not called angels.

They are called *nashiym* (women), as is the woman in the basket representing wickedness in verses 7 and 8. By contrast, the angel that Zechariah was speaking to is called a *malak*, a completely different word meaning "angel" or "messenger." The fact that the women have wings in Zechariah's vision might suggest angels to our minds, but we must be careful about going beyond what the text actually says.

Angel lore, myths, ancient stories, even personal encounters with guardian angels must be measured against an infallible standard, the Bible.

Worshiping or giving honor to a guardian angel is idolatry. *"Do not let anyone who delights in false humility and worship of angels disqualify you for the prize." (Colossians 2:18, NIV)*

NAME IT, CLAIM IT

Most Christians have heard some of the following: "You can have what you say," "The reason you haven't been healed is that you don't have enough faith," "We can write our own ticket with God if we decide what we want, believe that it's ours, and confess it," "He wants you rich and healthy," "What is the desire of your heart? Name it, claim it by faith, and it is yours! Your heavenly Father has promised it. It's right there in the Bible."

Such statements reflect the models which set forth a theology of the spoken word (*rhematology*) or of thought-actualization, commonly known as "positive confession", which stresses the inherent power of words and thoughts.

Some who teach this system argue that just as God, by His faith, spoke (or conceived of the creation in His mind) and matter came into existence (Genesis 1, Psalm 33:6, Hebrews 11:3, 2 Peter 3:5), so the Christian can speak (or conceive of things in his mind) and actually bring them into existence by faith.

There are many areas where name it and claim it departs from Biblical Christianity. The teaching really exalts man and his "faith" above God. In fact, many of the more extreme Word of Faith teachers teach that man was created on terms of equality with God and that man is the same class of being that He is Himself. This dangerous and heretical teaching denies the very basic tenets of Biblical Christianity, which is why the extreme proponents of the name it and claim it teaching must be considered to be cultic and not truly Christian.

Both the metaphysical cults and the name it and claim it teaching distort the truth and embrace the false teaching that our thoughts control reality. Whether it is the power of positive thinking or the prosperity gospel, the premise is the same—what you think or believe will happen is ultimately what controls what *will* happen. If you think negative thoughts or are lacking in faith, you will suffer or not get what you want. But on the other hand, if you think positive thoughts or just have "enough faith," then you can have health, wealth, and happiness now. This false teaching appeals to one of man's most basic instincts, which is one reason why it is hugely popular.

While the prosperity gospel and the idea of controlling one's future with his thoughts or faith is appealing to sinful man, it is insulting to a sovereign God who has revealed Himself in Scripture. Instead of recognizing the absolute sovereign power of God as revealed in the Bible, the name it and claim it adherents embrace a false god who cannot operate apart from their faith. They present a false view of God by teaching that He wants to bless you with health, wealth, and happiness but cannot do so unless YOU have enough faith. Thereby God is no longer in control but man is. Of course, this is completely antithetical to what Scripture teaches. God does not depend upon man's "faith" to act. Throughout Scripture we see God blessing whom He chooses to bless and healing whom He chooses to heal.

For what will it profit a man if he gains the whole world and forfeits his soul? Or what shall a man give in return for his soul?" (Matthew 16:24–26, NIV)

THEOPHOSTICS

The word "theophostic" comes from two Greek words which mean "God" and "light." Theophostic counseling is essentially "God bringing to light the truth." Theophostic counseling was originally developed by Dr. Ed Smith. The primary theory behind theophostic counseling is that many issues that require counseling, such as depression and anger, are based on falsehoods that a person believes based on comments made about them by others, errant teachings, and/or bad experiences in life.

The goal of theophostic counseling is to lead a person to Jesus for healing and allow Him to reveal the truth to the suffering person. Examples of this would be a young man who believes he was at fault for his parents' divorce, or a woman who experiences constant shame as a result of a sexual act she feels God will not forgive her of. Theophostic counseling seeks to reveal the lies and expose them to the truth that we are not responsible for the sinful actions of others and that God can and will forgive us and cleanse us of all of our sins.

In TPM, a Theophostic-trained facilitator asks the ministry recipient to drift back and identify the first memory he or she can remember in which was felt the same negative emotion that has been "triggered" in the present time and is the current source of trouble. The facilitator helps to identify a lie embedded in that memory, such as, "I'll never be safe." The recipient then prays to Jesus to reveal the truth with the expectation that both the lie and the emotional pain will be vanquished. "During Theophostic Prayer Ministry, demons sometimes masquerade as Jesus, appearing visually in people's minds looking like Jesus," warns Smith. But, don't be alarmed by this, he says, as it's easy to spot the demonic imposter. "I have found that when a person looks carefully at the face of a demon 'Jesus,' it will usually be dark or hazy, or look angry, scornful, or evil." Smith also warns against all forms of channeling or divining the future using TPM, because he admits that facilitators have used it for divination.

It is important to understand that "lie-based thinking" as defined by Smith is not addressed in the Bible. This category has nothing to do with what the Bible teaches about "the lie" which is in opposition to the gospel. When Jesus said "You shall know the truth and the truth shall set you free," he was referring to His objective teachings, not a mystical experience that regresses us back to childhood memories by our doing. There is no record anywhere in the Scriptures of a ministry that brings subjective revelations to a person's past memory and then changes how they interpret the memory.

This process is not "prayer" as defined Biblically. Prayer is not asking God for personal revelations about the meaning of first memory events. Prayer is not about getting revelations at all, it is about bringing our needs to God and knowing that He hears us. Furthermore, the process involves tempting God which the Bible prohibits. I say that because it is asking God to involve Himself in a process He has not ordained. The Bible tells us to forget what lies behind, not to reinterpret it. I do not agree with the view that we can do something that will get God to respond in some way. That is a pagan technique. It is not the same as normal prayer in which we make petitions to God and then trust Him as to the answers. We don't try to have an "encounter" or assume God will reveal something. This opens doors to the demonic and deeper deception.

THE THIRD EYE

The 3rd or Inner Eye – A metaphysical opening which refers to the 6th chakra (brow), that leads to higher consciousness. It is a New Age symbol of enlightenment. The Third Eye is a psychic ability connected to the occult. Dictionary.com defines occult as knowledge of secret or supernatural powers, beyond the range of ordinary senses, or secret/hidden information only available to the initiated. Next, we need to know how one "opens" this Third Eye. The main way that one opens himself up to the spirit realm, is through meditation. It is through meditation that one achieves an altered state of consciousness. Constantly, you will find that meditation, or the emptying of one's mind, is the doorway to all metaphysical activity.

Back to the 6th chakra. The chakras usually relate to Yoga, but not always. The 6th chakra in Yoga is the brow. When Kundalini (serpent power) rises to the brow, there is enlightenment that is characterized by light. Those using Yoga as a means of enlightenment get results by meditation, forced breathing patterns and using unnatural positions to force the power at the base of the spine upwards with the crown chakra as the main goal.

The third eye is also known as: The middle eye of Shiva in Buddhism.

In Hinduism it is the eye of clairvoyance. The Hindus wear the Tilak, which is the red spot between the brows. When I was researching, I looked at a link, describing Christian women who have been applying the red spot on their forehead and worshiping each other's divinity. In Egypt it is known as The Eye of Horus or the Eye of Osiris. In Freemasonry, it is the All Seeing Eye. This All Seeing Eye is found on our one dollar bill. This All Seeing Eye is surrounded by light.

But the eye usually means the same...esoteric knowledge that man so desires. This eye represents the passing into a spiritual world than man has no business entering. It is forbidden because it will deceive and oppress.

In Genesis 3:5-7 (KJV): *"For God doth know...then your eyes shall be opened and ye shall be as Gods...knowing Good and Evil.... And the eyes of them both opened."*

So for today...opening yourself up or opening your third eye is the same. It is opening a gate between two worlds which are the natural world and the demonic super-natural world. Meditation is a sure way of accomplishing this opening up of yourself especially through Contemplative prayer. This is simply meditation masked with Christian terminology. The fear that accompanies entrance into deep meditative levels is there for a reason...it is a warning from God.

If such a thing as a sixth sense or third eye truly exists, it is not of God. Those who claim to practice such abilities are either deceivers, self-deceived, and/or under the power of demonic forces. Leviticus 19:31 (NKJV) says, *"Do not rely on mediums and psychics, for you will be defiled by them. I, the Lord, am your God."* Consulting spiritists is foolish and angers the Lord (2 Chronicles 33:6). Acting as a medium or psychic was punishable by death in the Old Testament (Leviticus 20:27).

HYPNOTISM

Hypnosis involves the production of a state of mind usually induced by a procedure known as the hypnotic induction. The induction commonly involves a long series of preliminary instructions and suggestions. Hypnotic suggestions may be delivered by a hypnotist in the presence of the subject, or may be self-administered ("self-suggestion" or "auto-suggestion"). The words *'hypnosis'* and *'hypnotism'* both derive from the term *'neuro-hypnotism'* (nervous sleep). Deep trance can dramatically alter one's perception of reality, whether occasioned by traditional hypnosis, meditation, prayer, long term fasting, hypnotic religious rituals, or walking for miles in the hot desert. A popular misconception about hypnosis is that it involves a sleeping state, in which the subject is covertly forced to adopt thoughts and behaviors for which they would otherwise harbor an aversion. The trance-state is usually induced via hypnosis while the subject is wide awake; this state is known as the *'waking trance'* and it is the most common form of trance. Under this waking trance, it is unlikely that hypnosis alone can cause the subject to think and behave in a manner that is contrary to their moral constitution, for it is incapable of making a subject more gullible than they are when not in trance.

Subjects under hypnosis will usually remain acutely aware of their surroundings and may not even know that they are in the hypnotic state. The trance-state is a relaxing, slightly altered form of consciousness, which is very natural and commonly experienced by everyone, every day. During our favorite TV shows, driving down a long stretch of highway, or while washing the dishes, we all go into trance daily and we are seldom aware that we are in trance. Have you ever been in a daze while being asked questions by someone and you ended up asking them what you had just agreed to? Have you ever walked into a room to get something and then forgotten why you had entered that room, or what it was you were looking for? Because trance is so regularly experienced, it makes it hard to tell when we are going in and out of it. It is familiar to all of us.

There has been talk among Christians that hypnosis may open the mind to demonic influence. We don't know how this works, exactly, but it is possible. When a person's critical-thinking and decision making skills are turned off and their internal imagination cranked up, they are more susceptible to lies and harmful influences. This would seem to be a ripe time for a demonic attack. In fact, 1 Peter 5:8 warns us that we need to be self-controlled (make our own decision) and alert (think critically) to be protected against the enemy. And hypnosis has long been associated with those in the occult who want to reach evil spirits. This may even explain startlingly detailed "memories" that people wouldn't normally have (Acts 16:16-18). It's interesting to note how critical thinking and decision-making skills guard what comes into the mind in light of Proverbs 4:23 (NIV): *"Above all else, guard your heart, for everything you do flows from it."* When we put the guards to sleep, our hearts are left undefended, which directly influences our actions. Even if the hypnotist is working for our benefit, the risk of danger is phenomenal. The Bible validates this. Galatians 5:22-23 mentions that we need to control ourselves, not give control to someone else. Romans 6:12-13 says we need to submit ourselves to God, not someone else. Romans 6:16 warns us against submitting our decisions to another. Despite the success stories, despite how much we may trust the hypnotist, the Bible tells us to stay away from anyone trying to control our minds.

NOTES

Bible Scripture Translations: ESV-KJV-NASB-NIV-NKJV-NLT

Chris Lawson: "Do Christian Leaders Understand the Contemplative Prayer Movement"

Let Us Reason Ministries: Christian Yoga

Let Us Reason Ministries: A Great Compromise

The Discerning Sheep: Truth About Soaking Prayer

Berean Research: Sozo-Dangerous Inner Healing

Bill Randles: Wordpress/Meaning of Spiritual Drunkenness

Andrew Strom: Kundalini Awakening

Charisma News: Popular Meditation Thread

Jonas Clark: Prayer Meditation Labyrinths

Fanatic for Jesus: Heavenly Portals

Gotquestions.org: Out of Body Experience

Gotquestions.org: Angel Orbs

Women of Grace: Discerning Manifestations

Gotquestions.org: Gold Dust/What is Christian Mysticism

Letusreason.org: Yoga

Gotquestions.org: Psychics

Carm.org: Palm Reading

The Last Hiker/Wordpress.com: Young Living and Doterra New Age

Gotquestions.org: Karma

Bible.org: Reincarnation

Gotquestions.org: Christ Consciousness

Gotquestions.org: Holistic Medicine

Youthapologeticsindex.com: Grave Sucking

Gotquestions.org: Grave Sucking

Deceptioninthechurch.org: Dangers of Divination

www.ingramcontent.com/pod-product-compliance
Ingram Content Group UK Ltd.
Pitfield, Milton Keynes, MK11 3LW, UK
UKHW022222230426
12048UKWH00016BA/999